TO M... ALL THE BEST ... 1/16/18 (handwritten)

ABSOLUTE PITCH

THE SECRET TO GAINING PHENOMENAL
PERFORMANCE AND CUSTOMER ENCORES

ROBERT BLAHA

BRUCE THOMPSON

ABSOLUTE PITCH PUBLISHING

Printed in the United States of America

First Printing, 2017

ISBN 0-9992881-0-5

Absolute Pitch Publishing

1155 Kelly Johnson Blvd.

Colorado Springs, CO 80920

Robert Blaha — rblaha-hcaleadership@hca.com

Bruce Thompson — B.Thompson@slt-llc.com

www.AbsolutePitchBook.com

To our families

CONTENTS

PREFACE

Why We Wrote This Book

For almost thirty years we have watched organizations around the world struggle with the concepts of Lean, Six Sigma, Process Improvement, and a ton of ever-evolving improvement ideas. In that time, one thing has remained clear:

Everyone is looking for a simple method to get every person in an organization on the same page.

Absolute Pitch is that method. It can be explained quickly and briefly. People just "get it." You will find its simplicity and ease of application refreshing. Most important, you will find it doable.

You won't have to decode a complicated series of methodologies. That's because Absolute Pitch presents a straightforward idea: Let's get everyone in the organization hitting the right note at the right time so that everyone has a phenomenal experience.

In the time it takes to fly from Chicago to Philadelphia, you will find out why and how to make organizations more efficient, people more engaged, and customers call for encores.

So sit back, enjoy the melody of Absolute Pitch, and gain the tools you need to get people working together and achieving exceptional results.

ABSOLUTE PITCH

"Sorry I'm late," said Dan as he took his place at the table. It was a phrase he heard himself saying all too often these days. He was passionate about serving on the board of a local nonprofit, but tonight it felt like a miracle that he'd made it to the meeting at all. Things were tough at the company where he had worked for five years. Just as the organization had grown and his role had expanded, suddenly there always seemed to be someone coming to his door to report a problem or a major crisis.

Dan felt like the company was heading toward either a breakthrough moment or a breakdown. So, like many of the staff he supervised, he was working long, long hours—and feeling stressed most of the time—simply trying to deal with the crises. The rest of the folks mostly just clocked in and clocked out, going through the motions or looking for another job.

He fought the urge to check his phone for a response to an e-mail he'd sent to one of his department heads before rushing out of the office. Across the table, Michael gave him a reassuring nod hello. Dan was glad Michael was on the board, because he was the *kind of guy who always got things done. A couple of decades older than Dan, he had built up a technology company from scratch that was going from strength to strength. He radiated a calm authority, and Dan always got the sense that he had a deep satisfaction with his life. Somehow he always seemed to have time not only to run a thriving, big company but also to do the things he loved.*

How did Michael do it? Was it all down to luck? Or timing? He could just be one of those people who always seemed to be in the right place at the right time. Maybe there was some unique quality he had that made him a natural-born leader. Or perhaps charisma was the key.

At the end of the meeting, the two men caught each other up on work and life as they walked to their cars. As Michael stopped to show Dan pictures on his phone of his fly-fishing vacation with his daughter and grandchildren, Dan finally asked him, "How do you do it?"

"How do I do what?" said Michael, stopping in the parking lot, a wry grin on his face. "I can teach you how to fly-fish, but I'm guessing that's not what's on your mind."

"I can't even remember the last time I had a proper vacation with my family," said Dan. "The company you've built is so much bigger than the operations I run. There are so many more moving parts, so many more things that could go wrong. Yet I don't see you jumping from one crisis to the next."

Michael chuckled. "Daniel, my friend, if only it had always been this way," he said. "Believe me, there were times I felt as though I was digging myself out of a mountain of troubles in my business, and there was no way I would ever be able to dig fast enough."

"Look, tell me if I'm overstepping here," said Dan, "but do you think you could share with me what changes you made personally and at your company to be where you are now?"

Michael thought about it for a moment and smiled. "Better than that, I can show you," he said.

"When would you like me at your offices? Just name the time," replied Dan.

"No, no, I'm not going to drag you around on a company tour," said Michael. "But I do need a couple of evenings of your time, no distractions, okay?" Dan usually caught up on work at night, but he nodded. This was an important opportunity.

That was how Dan had found himself, smartly dressed, in a very unlikely place one night the next week: a crowded concert hall, at a performance by their city's symphony orchestra. "Classical music?" Dan had said to his wife, Jill, as they got ready to go out. "I wanted to find out how to turn my business around!" Deep down, he knew that Michael must have a good reason for suggesting a night of symphony. His hesitation was more about feeling out of his depth. Dan's knowledge of music pretty much began and ended with the metal bands he'd listened to in college.

So, he was surprised and delighted to find that it was a great night of entertainment. The orchestra played well, and at the end, Dan joined the rest of the audience in clapping enthusiastically. He looked over at the smiling faces of Jill, Michael, and his wife, Carol, and then gazed around at the rows of happy faces in the crowd.

When the applause died down and everyone got up from their seats, Dan said to Michael, "Thanks, that was great. I had no idea we had such a talented orchestra here in our own town." He waited for Michael to give him some clue as to what any of this had to do with improving his business, but Michael only handed him two more tickets—to a performance at the same time the following week, at the same place, but by a different orchestra, which was touring from a major city.

"That's not just any orchestra," Jill told him later. "It's one of the Big Five."

"The big what?"

"Just trust me. They'll be amazing."

The following week, Dan was still skeptical. He couldn't tell the difference between Bach and Beethoven, let alone one orchestra from another. Yet from the moment the conductor raised the baton, something extraordinary happened. A hush fell over the concert hall. It was as if Dan could actually feel the audience's expectation in the air. And as the baton came down to start the symphony, every single person in that concert hall was swept up in the performance—each individual player and audience member, the conductor, and even the composer, whose presence could be felt through the music. Time flew by, and when the final note sounded, the audience erupted in applause and whistles and jumped to their feet.

Like everyone else, Dan left the concert hall on a high. It was only when they were having coffee afterward and Michael said, "Ladies, would you excuse us for a moment?" that he started to come down to earth. Dan and Michael shifted their chairs a little to one side as their wives chatted.

"So, what did you think?" asked Michael.

"Wow, it was . . . well, you don't experience that level of excellence every day. And when you do, it just blows you away." He didn't want to seem ungrateful for the tickets for the previous week's performance though. "Don't get me wrong, last week was great. It's just that this concert was . . ." Dan trailed off, searching for the right words.

"They just knocked it out of the park, right?" said Michael.

And that's when it clicked, and Dan realized what Michael's intention had been.

"Imagine the success I could have in my business if we did for our customers what that orchestra just did for its audience," said Dan.

"Bingo!" replied Michael.

"But it was the same venue, same-sized orchestra, same style of music," said Dan. "What did they do that was so different?"

"Well, the difference is that last week's performance was pleasing, but tonight the orchestra achieved **Absolute Pitch**," Michael said.

Dan listened carefully as Michael explained. To achieve Absolute Pitch meant that all of the players in the orchestra had worked together in total harmony. They each had a clear understanding of the notes they had to play, and when. And because they fully understood how their part fitted into the whole, they were committed to achieving the shared goal of a perfect performance.

With a maestro for a conductor, they received the acknowledgment they needed, and they got the right signals to tell them when to slow down, speed up, or change their intensity to give the audience the optimal experience.

The members of each section—strings, brass, woodwind, percussion—worked together as a unit. And the sections were perfectly coordinated and synced so that they struck the right chords at the right time. Soloists came to the fore when they were needed and played in harmony with others when the composition required it.

The result was that every individual hit the right note at the right time, every time, and in unison. That was why it sounded perfect; that was why the audience got to their feet and shouted, "Encore! Encore!"

Absolute Pitch: When every member of an organization hits the right note every time, in unison and harmony. This results in encore performances.

"Of course, the orchestra didn't get to that level overnight, just like I wasn't able to turn things around in my business just like that," Michael said, clicking his fingers.

"What did you have to do?" Dan asked.

"We had to listen to what our consumers wanted, just like the orchestra had to engage with its audience. We had to refine our business strategies and plans—or our composition, if you will. We had to make sure that every individual knew the part they had to play, and we had to spend time rehearsing with one another, just like those musicians did before they got up on that stage tonight.

"I'm not going to tell you it always goes perfectly for us," Michael continued. "Sometimes things don't go as planned and there's a sour note—that's life. The difference is, we're much better now at getting back on Absolute Pitch. That's because we continually practice and make refinements. We continually listen for discord, so we can hear it more quickly than before—and we can fix it faster.

"And because everybody is pulling in the same direction now, they're hitting the right notes more often than not," he said.

"That's why your customers keep asking for more," said Dan.

"And I've got to tell you, our shareholders and employees are pretty happy with the situation, too," said Michael, smiling.

As this book unfolds, we will be checking back in with Dan to see his progress on working toward Absolute Pitch with Michael's guidance. And as Michael reveals the principles of Absolute Pitch to Dan, we will take you through them step by step so that you can start working toward Absolute Pitch in any organization and start getting standing ovations from your audience.

A Note About Terms

Don't worry, you won't need to enroll in a music appreciation course to understand this book. We have made a point of using simple terms that can be applied universally to all types of organizations.

Organization: Any group with a common purpose—for instance, a small or medium-sized business, large corporation, government body, hospital, school, church, nonprofit, or social or community group.

Customers: The people who acquire an organization's products or services. Customers include people who buy from businesses and people who access the products or services of a nonprofit organization free of charge.

Consumers: The people who use an organization's products or services.

Stakeholders: People who have something at stake in the organization. For a company, this may mean shareholders or owners. For other organizations, it may mean people who are impacted by the organization, such as community members.

What Absolute Pitch Means for Your Organization

Absolute Pitch is a new methodology of organizational excellence that focuses on establishing and maintaining harmony among the individuals and teams that make up an organization, while getting them to move in sync with consumers' needs and deliver value to stakeholders. It requires getting everybody—the individuals in an organization, its customers and consumers, and its stakeholders—on the same page, on the same note, on the same pitch.

The goal of these methods is to create an organization in which every individual knows exactly what they need to do and is committed to performing their role perfectly because they know their efforts will contribute to something greater. An Absolute Pitch organization brings out the best in every individual because they know they are helping to create a symphony that is pleasing not only to them as individuals but to the people who are listening.

The result is that everyone—customers, consumers, stakeholders, and the organization itself—gets a phenomenal experience from start to finish. The organization is able to offer a better product or service, and a superior overall experience, and this gives them the edge over competitors.

Imagine what that could mean for your business's profits. Or imagine how it could change the way you feel about going to your workplace in the morning. Or if you're involved in a community group, a nonprofit, or the parents' association at your child's school, imagine how much more you could achieve if every single one of you was doing the right thing at the right time, every time.

The truth is, most organizations never even *try* for Absolute Pitch, let alone achieve it. Yet any organization can make it a reality by following the methods outlined in the following chapters. So let's get started!

2

COMPOSING THE SYMPHONY

The office had gradually fallen quiet as everyone left one by one, and just Dan remained, sitting in the circle of light cast by his desk lamp. He leaned back and took what felt like his first deep breath of the day.

It had been a week or so since Michael had introduced him to the concept of Absolute Pitch, when he had witnessed the excellence that could be achieved when people worked perfectly in concert with one another. But when he imagined himself standing in the maestro's shoes, getting the people in his company to change the tune they were playing, he balked. He was unsure how to proceed, especially in the pressure-cooker conditions of an average day.

One thing Dan knew for sure: he and his staff couldn't keep going the way they had been. As the operations manager of a company that designed and built medical devices, there was a lot on the line. Six months earlier, they had received regulatory approval to start selling in two major markets, and he knew that each moment of delay meant lost revenue and coveted market share. Dan wasn't sure exactly how far behind schedule they were running; he just knew that some excuses were going to have to be made.

The state of Absolute Pitch the symphony orchestra had achieved was beginning to seem almost like a dream. Dan felt a pang of urgency that made him sit up straight. Something told him he needed to act soon. Michael had shown him what was possible, but if Dan didn't find a way to begin steering his department in that direction now, the dream might just fade away.

He picked up his phone, scrolled through his contacts list, and called Michael.

"So, you're ready then!" Michael's excitement was evident as he answered the phone; obviously he'd expected Dan to call and ask for some more guidance. "What have you done so far?"

Dan took a beat before confessing that he hadn't instituted any major changes to his teams' performance yet.

"Great!" said Michael, much to Dan's surprise. He quickly continued: "Let me explain by giving you an example. Imagine the London Philharmonic has sold out a performance at Carnegie Hall."

"Okay."

"*But they haven't prepared for it. They haven't practiced their parts. They haven't gotten together to rehearse. They don't even know what composition the conductor has chosen,*" said Michael. "*Actually, while the crowd is finding their seats, the composer is backstage with a pencil, scribbling down the end of the symphony.*"

"*Uh-huh,*" said Dan uncertainly.

"*Just wouldn't happen, would it?*" asked Michael.

"*Well, I'd certainly hope not.*"

"*So it's the last thing you should do either,*" Michael replied. "*Having said that, I see organizations do it all the time. They throw themselves into the performance without doing the preparation, and then they wonder why they're not getting encores.*"

Dan could immediately think of many experiences he'd had as a customer dealing with staff who were meant to be helping him but were obviously unclear on what role they were even meant to be playing. He could think of the times he'd tried to buy a product or hire a service when it quickly became clear that people at the company weren't getting on with each other or seemed to be working off different scripts. Speaking to one department, he might get one answer and then a completely different answer when he spoke to another.

He thought about the teams whose work he oversaw. There were a couple of people who could hardly bear to work with the rest of their team. And then other divisions at his company often seemed to be following a different beat than his people anyway. Altogether, they were not on the same beat as the clients who ordered medical devices, the doctors and nurses who used them, or the shareholders of the company.

"I have some work to do, don't I?" said Dan.

"Yes, yes, you do," Michael replied. "Every maestro has some work to do before walking out on stage."

At the symphony, when the conductor raises the baton, it's the sign that everybody is ready for a superb performance—the players, the conductor, the audience. As Dan has just learned, much work has to go on behind the scenes before that moment. From our experience in guiding businesses toward Absolute Pitch, we know that these are the steps he will need to take to ensure everyone is fully prepared in his organization:

Setting the Stage

Before an orchestra takes the stage, there are practical issues to address. The right players, and the right number of players, need to be selected, depending on the music to be played. Their seats need to be arranged in a way that enables them to play optimally together, in a venue that has good acoustics and is comfortable for the audience. The players and their instruments all need to get to the venue in time. There has to be a way for the audience to hear about the upcoming performance, purchase tickets, and get there.

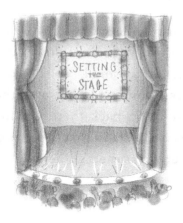

The principle is the same in any organization. For instance, at Dan's company, a number of factors should have been in place before they began ramping up production to sell in the two new markets where they had won regulatory approval. The organization needed the right number of manufacturing and support staff. Raw materials had to be sourced from several locations. A decision needed to be made about where production would take place, which turned out to be at multiple sites in different states and other countries. Transportation and lines of communication had to be worked out.

Dan's company—like many organizations—didn't take the time to get these basics right before they started, so they had to make it up as they went along. But those aiming for Absolute Pitch take this phase of preparation seriously. They carefully think through all of the logistics first, rather than solving issues as they arise.

Establish the Tempo

Nobody enjoys hearing music that's the wrong tempo for their mood. For instance, you've just sat down for a quiet meal and good conversation in a small, softly lit restaurant when thumping pop music comes blaring over the speakers. You're probably not likely to go back there anytime soon. Absolute Pitch organizations understand that to get encores, they need to move at the same tempo as their audience.

Tempo: The pace at which an organization needs to move in order to meet its consumers' demands.

No matter what sort of organization you're in, people consume the goods or services you provide at a certain rate. It might be a particular number of products that leave store shelves in an average week. If you provide a service, perhaps you need to see a client every thirty minutes to keep up with the number of people coming through your doors. For a nonprofit, the metric might be the number of people who require assistance each day.

No matter what type of consumer demand we're talking about, if your organization doesn't deliver goods or services at that pace, it's not pleasing to your consumers, your organization, or your stakeholders. It certainly doesn't lead to encores.

Reward Ensemble Performances

Before the financial crisis of 2007, a number of bankers figured out a way to sell mortgages to people who wouldn't normally qualify for loans because they didn't have enough income or assets. These subprime mortgages were a method of selling things to people who could never really pay for them. The bankers who sold the mortgages to homeowners—and then sold the debts to other financial institutions—made a lot of money.

Of course, their actions turned out to be disastrous not just for their own organizations but for the entire economy when homeowners started defaulting on their loans. Those bankers were financially rewarded for doing something that was good for them as individuals yet bad for the whole.

Something like this would never happen in an organization that was on Absolute Pitch. Rather than putting the spotlight on "rock star" solo performances, Absolute Pitch organizations measure and reward how well the individual contributes to the whole. This is also what a symphony orchestra does, because in such a large ensemble of musicians it is vital that every player is working toward one shared aim: a perfect performance.

Ensemble performance: When an individual performs in a way that contributes to and benefits the whole organization.

Your organization's results are the sum total of all individual contributions, so your success depends on people consistently behaving in ways that benefit the whole organization. Every time an individual is faced with a choice—should I do A, or should I do B?—that person needs to choose the course of action that is best for the organization. Every time.

When you reward people for a certain behavior, you get more of that behavior. So ask yourself: Are you rewarding behavior that contributes to the good of the whole organization? Are you rewarding people for making the right choices?

All too often, the systems and processes in place in an organization measure and reward exactly the wrong behavior that puts the individual first—sometimes at the expense of the whole organization. You may have seen examples of this in the workplace: Let's say it's late on a Friday, and someone rushes in to see the supervisor of the department to break the news that there's a big crisis. Someone failed to do something crucial, or they did something wrong. Now the quarterly report won't be finished by Monday morning or that order won't be ready for your most important client. But never fear, this superhero is going to rescue the company by working through the weekend to get it done!

In organizations that reward this kind of behavior, rock-star types thrive when there is disharmony because it gives them opportunities to go out and shine on center stage. In fact, it is within their interests to create further disharmony. And that's exactly what they do by jumping in to save the day. They may believe they're doing the right thing—but they're doing it on their own, out of step with the rest of the organization.

The rock star wins appreciation and recognition for going above and beyond the call of duty, even though their actions do not have a positive impact on the organization's overall performance in the long term.

Indeed, fixing the underlying problems that led to the immediate problem will require contributions from other people in the department and possibly other departments or the organization as a whole. It will require that a number of people take a time-out for rehearsals, which we're going to discuss in chapter 6.

Organizations get a much better result if they reward people when they behave not like rock stars but like members of an orchestra who see themselves as part of a team working in unison toward a perfect performance. Members of an orchestra are rewarded when they play their parts well and in harmony with the players in their own section and the orchestra as a whole. They aren't rewarded when they are off beat or off key—or when they jump up, throw away the sheet music, and play what they think is a better tune.

Compose a Symphony

Just as the musicians in an orchestra know the right notes to play because they have sheet music, individuals in an Absolute Pitch organization know the right choices to make because they have a composition to follow.

The composition tells everyone in an organization what actions they should take, when, and how in order to achieve the desired outcome. It sets the expectations for each person by providing guidelines on how they are to do their work. In a practical sense, the composition comprises the processes, methodologies, strategies, and tactics that people in an organization follow.

Composition: An organization's plan for how tasks will be performed.

Eventually, at Dan's company, they sorted out the logistics of making products for their new markets. They now had the staff they needed, and they had sorted out the locations of their manufacturing operations and their suppliers. But they were so busy patching all that together that they didn't spend enough time composing a plan for how the manufacturers and support staff would perform their work. Responsibilities were less than clear, as there were few procedures to guide workflow. Metrics and processes to measure their performance and their progress toward the end result had not been fully established, which is why Dan couldn't be sure exactly how far behind schedule they were. Nor was it clear how the teams of staff were to communicate with one another.

Imagine how many choices each of those personnel had to make at work each day. Without a composition to follow, how would they know whether it was in the company's best interest to choose option A or option B in a given situation? Without a composition, they simply had to choose what they thought was best, and that choice was often what benefited them as individuals rather than the organization as a whole. We can all guess the results: there was discord between individuals and between teams, and there were budget overruns and missed deadlines.

Now imagine what it would have been like if each of those individuals had been given the same criteria for making choices. They would know that when they were presented with a choice between A or B, the success of the company depended on them choosing A every time. They would know that if they chose B, they would take the organization off Absolute Pitch, and the symphony wouldn't sound pleasing. They would clearly understand the individual parts they were to play and how playing their parts would contribute to the whole organization's success. And they would know how they were to interact with the other members of their team and with the greater organization. With these systems and processes in place, everyone would be on the same page and there would be less chance of discord. There might even be an encore performance.

Always Be Prepared

So, the stage is set for work to commence—the right people are in the right places, and they have everything they need to get their jobs done. Each person in the organization knows the tempo at which they are going to work, so that together they match the tempo of their consumers. They have their composition: the game plan they're going to follow. Each person's part has been carefully scripted, so they know how to act; they know the right choices to make. They know how their individual performance contributes to the outcome for the whole organization. Communication lines have been established. Systems and processes are in place to orchestrate how the members in each team interact with one another and how the teams interact with the whole organization. The audience has been prepared too. They have a heightened expectation of your product or service. Within and outside of the organization, everyone is ready—the whole value stream is prepared.

Everyone's ready to pick up their instrument and play the right note at the right time when the baton comes down.

Absolute Pitch organizations know that preparation doesn't stop there, however. They know they need to continually make sure that the organization is in a state of readiness. They listen carefully for sour notes while the symphony is under way. When they hear them, they take time for rehearsals; they fine-tune the composition until everyone is on Absolute Pitch, playing a tune that is pleasing to everyone's ears.

A Hospital Unit Fine-Tunes Its Composition

Since Dan had been going deeper into Absolute Pitch with Michael, he was beginning to observe examples of the principles everywhere he went. This time, it happened at a hospital.

Having had a minor procedure a few months before, Dan had returned for a checkup. As he walked to his appointment, he wasn't looking forward to being back in the same treatment room. The previous time, he had been there for ages waiting for the doctor. His eyes had kept returning to a chart on the wall: "Hand-Cleaning Compliance."

At first, Dan had been shocked that anyone would even think it was necessary to measure hand-cleaning compliance in a hospital. Wasn't it a given that every staff member would clean their hands? When he walked over to read the chart more carefully, he was even more shocked: in this unit, the goal was 80 percent compliance. It took a moment for it to sink in that they actually considered it acceptable for one in five staff to fail to clean their hands. Dan certainly didn't consider it acceptable.

Now that he was coming to grips with Absolute Pitch, he was able to recognize his earlier hospital experience for what it was: a sour note. Hand-cleaning is a choice people make, Dan thought. When one in five people failed to make that choice, they were failing to play the music correctly. They were not hitting the right note every time. And by putting a chart on the wall showing that there was only 80 percent compliance, the hospital seemed to be telling staff and patients that it was okay. At the very least, Dan decided, on this visit he was going to ask them to take that sign down.

He was pleasantly surprised when he was shown into the treatment room. Instead of a chart reminding him of the staff's less-than-

perfect hand-cleaning compliance, the first thing he noticed was a new hand sanitizer dispenser. It was strategically located so that in order to get to the patient, a staff member had to come face-to-face with the dispenser. Dan had to wait for the doctor—unfortunately that part of the hospital experience hadn't improved—so he went into the corridor and poked his head into a few vacant treatment rooms and saw they were all set up this way now.

Dan's wife is a designer, and he remembered something she often said: People are like water; they will always take the easiest path. With a slight redesign, the hospital had made it easy and natural for every staff member to make the right choice every time. It was clear to Dan that someone had really thought this through. They had created an environment where people knew exactly what they were expected to do.

When a nurse came by to take Dan's vitals, he asked her about the setup. He learned that the changes had been brought in about a month before. "It's been amazing," said the nurse. "Since we got these dispensers, I have never seen a doctor or a nurse forget to make sure their hands are clean." A side benefit was now that they had 100 percent compliance, the hospital wasn't wasting time and money checking up on how often everyone cleaned their hands.

Most important to the nurse was that she truly felt her efforts were contributing to a better overall outcome for everybody: the people she worked with, the hospital as a whole, and of course the patients, their families, and the communities in which they lived. Her experience was the equivalent of an individual musician playing her part in a symphony that was pleasing to everyone's ears. As an audience member, to Dan's ears, it certainly sounded a whole lot better. In fact, he might even recommend this hospital to friends and family now.

3

GETTING IN UNISON

W hen Michael learned that before Dan got so busy with his job and three kids, he had been a keen fly-fisherman, Michael insisted that their next catch-up had to be at his favorite stream on a Saturday afternoon. Under a blue sky, the sun glinting off the crystal clear water, the two men stood talking, fishing, and laughing.

Dan couldn't help but laugh as he described a situation he was dealing with at work, realizing how absurd and wasteful of people's time and energy it was. At one of the company's manufacturing facilities, lounge suites had been purchased and were to be installed in the factory.

"Lounges," said Michael, deadpan. "In a factory."

"And not just any lounges. We're talking really big, luxurious ones, like you'd see in a swank hotel lobby," Dan replied. "Granted, the manager thinks he's doing the right thing. He says people are working such long hours, they actually need these lounges to rest on during their breaks."

"While all you're wondering is how you got to the point where people need naps?"

Dan nodded. "The thing is, the idea's causing a lot of friction with other teams in the company. They've caught wind of it and feel like the factory workers are getting special treatment. Can you imagine explaining a bunch of cushy lounge suites to a customer who happens to turn up to find out why their order is running late?"

"Can you do something about it?" Michael asked.

"Look, it seems self-evident to me that it's not a great decision. But it's tough to veto it without looking like the bad guy," said Dan. "No matter whether the guys in the factory get their chairs or not, it seems as though someone can argue the case that it was the wrong decision." Dan fell silent. The only sounds were the water gently running and a bird calling in the distance.

Finally, Michael spoke. "So, if we think about it in terms of Absolute Pitch, it's pretty simple."

"Simple?"

"Well, everyone should be on the same page of the composition about this, shouldn't they? There is a clear-cut decision to be made: lounges or no lounges. In an Absolute Pitch organization, everyone knows the right choice to make, and every time there's a choice to make, they make the right one."

"But that's just it: how do you get people to agree on what the right choice is?" asked Dan, having a hard time hiding his exasperation.

"I'm going to guess your company's got a vision and values statement," Michael replied.

"Of course. I was there a couple of years back when they brought in a team of advisers to come up with some new wording that better summed up the mission of the company."

"What's it say?"

"Well, it's . . . it's to, to take pride in making a positive outcome for our stakeholders, and . . ." Dan trailed off. "You'd think I'd be able to remember it given I walk past it in the hall about twenty times a day."

"I'll bet there were a lot of hours and a lot of dollars spent on perfecting that mission statement so that it sounds just right," said Michael. "Yet it leaves everybody cold."

"Uh-huh."

"I'll also bet the sentiments have never truly become a part of how people work."

"I have to admit, you're right," Dan replied.

"And there is your answer, my friend. People are having a hard time agreeing on what the right choice is because they're not all facing the same direction; they're not all sharing the same vision," said Michael just as his line went taut. He grinned and began reeling in.

In an organization that has reached Absolute Pitch, something rare happens: everyone has a clear understanding of the organization's vision, and it is ingrained in the decisions they make each day. You can ask anybody in the organization to step forward—an executive, a part-time employee, a volunteer—and they will be able to tell you the organization's purpose and the values that guide their actions. This clarity extends beyond the organization itself: ask a customer, consumer, or stakeholder, and they too will be able to articulate what the organization delivers, what it stands for, and how it conducts itself.

For a symphony orchestra, the equivalent is when every musician in every seat has total clarity on the symphonic outcome they are aiming for and the way in which they will achieve it, as do the audience members and the stakeholders, such as the local community or benefactors who support the orchestra.

It is uncommon to see an orchestra or any other organization achieve such clarity of vision. But when it happens, it is unique and special—and it commands an encore performance.

Asking "What's in It for Me?"

For a performance to be considered on Absolute Pitch, everyone—customers, consumers, stakeholders, and members of the organization—has to have an exceptional experience. So when the members of an Absolute Pitch organization sit down to seek clarity on their vision, they explore and discuss what each group values most.

The members of an **organization** need to ask themselves what they value the most about being a part of the organization. There are many different ways they can ask this question, but in essence they're asking the WIIFM question: "What's in it for me?"

In a workplace, part of the WIIFM is a paycheck, of course. People come to work each day so they can support themselves and their families. But all organizations, including businesses, can dig deeper than that level. To get to the bottom of why people contribute to an organization, the first question is: Why does our organization exist?

For a nonprofit, the answer may be relatively obvious—for instance, a soup kitchen exists to feed the hungry; an animal shelter is there to find homes for abandoned or abused pets. But the question is equally relevant for businesses and can be the catalyst for some very interesting discussions. Every business does something that is important from a big-picture point of view. For instance, a company that manufactures headphones might discover that the fundamental reason they make their product is to improve people's lives. When a company that provides house-cleaning services looks deeper, they may realize that ultimately they contribute to happier families.

To get to the core of what the members of the organization most value, they should also ask themselves: What is it about our roles that we like? Frequently people say they value things like feeling respected, working in a fun environment, being with their coworkers, being part of something bigger, or taking pride in their work.

The organization also needs to consider what the **customer** and **consumer** value about their products or services. The customer may value things such as affordability, helpful customer service, an easy ordering process, and good guarantee and return policies. For the consumer who uses the product or service, the main drivers might be quality, reliability, appearance, and functionality.

The **stakeholders** of a business are its shareholders, and they value profit. Nonprofit organizations, which don't have to please shareholders, still need to determine what matters most to other people who have an interest in the organization's activities. For instance, donors might value that a nonprofit is achieving good outcomes for the people it aids; community members might value a school for involving parents in decision-making or helping to make their neighborhood a great place to live.

Establishing a Unison of Values in Decision-Making

Once an Absolute Pitch organization has spent time determining what the members of the organization, customers, consumers, and stakeholders value, these values then become their criteria for making decisions.

It's not enough for the organization to just consider what the customers want. Nor should decisions be made based solely on what customers, consumers, stakeholders, or the individuals within the organization desire. Every decision needs to be made in unison according to what is valued by all parties.

> **Unison:** People in an organization working in sync with one another and in alignment with the values of the organization, customers, consumers, and stakeholders.

Dan's company still has some work to do to get clarity on everyone's values. Only then will they be able to align their decisions to the WIIFM of all concerned. When it comes to the installation of plush lounge chairs, it is easy to see what's in it for the employees at the factory. But is it of value to the customers who pay for the medical devices the company produces? Is it of value to the consumers, the nurses and doctors who use the devices when treating patients? And to the shareholders of the company? Obviously not.

If Dan's company had clarity of values, a decision-making process that was causing discord would have been straightforward. They would have known that if they approved the lounge chairs, their decision would align with the values of only the employees of the factory, not the organization as a whole, let alone their customers, consumers, and shareholders. It would have been immediately clear that the answer should be "no."

An organization will never attain Absolute Pitch if it suboptimizes one group at the expense of another—for instance, if Dan's company puts its factory employees ahead of the whole company and its customers, consumers, and stakeholders. Similarly, the company will be off Absolute Pitch if it makes decisions that benefit only the shareholders, customers, or consumers at the expense of its employees.

Another way to look at this is to imagine an orchestra that spends almost its entire annual budget on attracting the finest string and woodwind players in the world and then fails to invest in the brass or percussion sections. What is the experience going to be like for the musicians? What is it going to sound like to the audience? How will it sound to the orchestra's benefactors?

Using Clarity of Vision to Drive Cultural Change

Trying to change the culture in an organization can seem like an overwhelming task. But once you have done the work to achieve clarity of vision, you have at your disposal a highly effective tool for positive change.

An important part of Absolute Pitch is regular rehearsal— that is, taking time out of your day-to-day work to fine-tune your performance. During that rehearsal time, a clearly articulated vision can be used to identify the behavioral changes you need to make to create the organization you want. For instance, let's say discussions have revealed that one of the main reasons people participate in your organization is to feel respected. As everyone is in agreement that respect is important, the question now becomes: How do we show our respect for one another? One way is to be sure to say "thank you." It's easy to do, and it creates a culture of respect. So a decision could be made that everyone will practice this simple behavior.

As another example, perhaps everyone has agreed that one of the things they value the most is to feel that they're part of a learning organization. They don't want to keep making the same mistakes over and over again but instead want to learn from their experiences. How might you make learning a part of your culture? Learning starts with reflecting on your experiences: you take stock of what you did, what worked, and what you could do better. So one way to create a learning culture would be to schedule time for regular reflection and make it easy for everyone to share what they have learned.

To achieve lasting improvements in an organization's culture, behavioral changes such as these need to be reinforced continually until they become a part of the way everyone does their daily work. This requires leaders to keep drawing attention back to the values that have been identified as most important to the organization. Everyone needs to be regularly reminded of why they are there and how they should act. Then the organization's vision will become much more than just well-written words on a hallway sign. They will be part of the fabric of the organization, intertwined in everything people do.

Tapping into Your Greater Purpose

Cast your mind back to an exceptional performance you once saw. Perhaps it was an amazing concert, a movie that left you speechless, or a football or baseball game in which a team played as close to perfect as you can imagine. You probably left feeling awesome for having attended. You also might have noticed that the people on the stage, screen, or field seemed to feel as elated as you. In fact, it's very difficult to imagine a musician, actor, or sports star giving a top performance unless they feel emotionally engaged in what they are doing. Their passion inspires everyone around them, and it has a positive impact on the audience.

Do you think this level of passion is something only great artists, athletes, and performers can experience? Think again. Any organization can help its individuals become fully engaged in what they do by uncovering the greater purpose of their work.

First let's look at the business world. The situation in most companies is that they have never brought everyone together to discuss what they value the most. That means there is no WIIFM beyond receiving a paycheck. People simply come to work every day and do what they do. They don't have criteria by which to make decisions, and the results of their decisions aren't measured. So they have no way to tell if they're making the right choices, and they go home at the end of the day not knowing whether they had a positive impact on the company. In fact, often the only feedback they get is when something goes wrong. Is it any wonder that employees in such a company are there in body but not in mind or spirit?

When a company identifies the greater purpose of its work, it taps into what enriches the lives of its employees. As a result, it gets not only their body but their mind and spirit too. They become emotionally engaged in their work.

There are simple, effective techniques for reminding employees that they are doing more than just paying their bills when they come to work each day. For instance, when employees are brought together for a meeting, instead of going straight to the usual PowerPoint graphs and charts, a unifying image might be projected on the screen that reminds everyone of the reason they are there. A hospital might use an image of a child undergoing treatment. A defense contractor might show a picture of a soldier in a foreign battlefield. Immediately, this visual reminder of the company's greater purpose gets everyone on the same page. It focuses their attention on solving the issues that are truly important, rather than getting caught up in concerns that take them off Absolute Pitch.

Let's think about the experiences of the employees in these companies. Perhaps in the past they went home every day not knowing if their work made a positive impact because the only time their supervisors gave them feedback was when they made a mistake. Imagine the difference in their performance when they are shown that what they're doing is important and people are counting on them to do their job well. In the hospital, staff know that if they excel at their work, they might save more lives. The employees on the factory floor at the defense contractor know that because they are there to "turn a wrench," servicemen and -women are going to get what they need to make the country safer.

When employees see the bigger picture and feel good about their contribution at work, it's an uplifting experience for them. The more positive their experience is, the more they want to repeat it tomorrow—and every day after that. Improvement leads to further improvement, because employees feel so good about the positive impact they've already had, they want more. It creates a desire within the company for encore performances. And when you can capture that feeling in your organization, you are on the way to Absolute Pitch.

~

A Bold Mission Guides a Nonprofit to Exceptional Results

Dan got a sense of fulfillment from sitting on the board of the local nonprofit where he had met Michael. The organization operated a food pantry for the needy, and their services always seemed to be in demand.

This month, Dan had made sure to clear his schedule to get to the board meeting on time because a special guest had been invited to give a presentation. It was a good friend of Michael's who was visiting from Colorado, where he led a nonprofit foster care and adoption organization called Hope & Home. Their goal was to get children out of the traditional foster-care system into loving homes. They were doing such a good job that Michael had asked his friend Ross to share the organization's story with the board in the hopes that it might help them as they charted a course for their organization.

"In the nonprofit world, there are a handful of organizations that stand out because they do a better job of articulating their purpose and inspiring their members to give it everything they've got," said Michael as he stood to introduce Ross. "These organizations attain a level of excellence that sets them apart from others in their field. Hope & Home is one such organization."

As Michael handed the floor to Ross, a picture of a family sitting happily together at a dinner table came up on the screen behind him. Dan had heard about the cold realities of life for children in the traditional foster-care system. It gave him a sense of hope to see these children getting the love they needed, just like his own kids at home.

Ross explained to the board that when the organization was established in 1998, they had set out with a clear mission: to reduce the number of children in standard institutional care and to improve the quality of their care by raising the standards that foster and adoptive parents must meet. Bluntly, he said, Hope & Home's focus was to move kids who were stuck in traditional foster care with its mercenary approach, to a better environment founded on a mission-driven approach.

Unified by this purpose, individuals within the organization achieved extraordinary results. Against all odds, in less than two decades they had begun to significantly improve the care received by children in the foster-care system. Previously, many of these children were a forgotten underclass, provided little more than a roof over their heads.

Hope & Home's success was due to several factors, he explained. From the outset they had worked to create excellent lines of communication, processes, systems, and a sense of teamwork. Another factor that distinguished it from other organizations providing the same services was the degree to which everyone was engaged in their work and committed to doing their best. They couldn't wait to get to work because they knew they were providing a higher standard of service than others and were having a greater impact. The staff may not have been paid more than at other child-placement agencies, but because of their passion, they gave a lot more.

This meant the organization could achieve more, often with fewer staff than other organizations. And because they were getting results, they received more state attention and funding, which in turn enabled them to make further improvements. The excellence of their work had been recognized with many awards, and Ross had been invited to speak at numerous conferences and sit on influential boards and committees. This gave Hope & Home a stronger voice in decision-making about the foster-care system.

Everybody was winning in this scenario, thought Dan. The people who worked at Hope & Home loved what they did. Foster and adoptive parents received exceptional support, and children had a better quality of life and a brighter future. This benefited their communities and the state as a whole. Because the organization had attained clarity of vision, they were in unison: their work was aligned with the values of the organization, the foster children and parents, and the local and wider community.

From the way Ross described it, another crucial part of their success was that individuals were working harmoniously together. Harmony was something that was sorely lacking in Dan's company. It was certainly something he wanted to know more about.

4

HARMONIZING THE ORGANIZATION

D an could not remember hearing anything quite like it before in his life. Sweet and rich, the sound of the choir reverberated around the room. One of the women on the board of his nonprofit had managed to secure them as an act for their annual fund-raising gala concert. It was a fantastic choice, as the audience was transfixed.

He was witnessing something amazing, Dan realized. Their voices were coming together in such a way that they created something much more powerful than a mere group of individuals singing at the same time. The result was a sound that was almost like something from another world. What was the secret? How did they do it?

Dan watched the conductor closely for a moment, observing how she used her hands and, in fact, her whole body to convey to the singers the tempo she wanted them to hit and the qualities she wanted to draw out of their voices.

Then, as he looked from one singer to the next, he noticed that it wasn't just a one-way communication. It was as if an invisible web connected the whole choir as one entity. Each performer would glance down at their music, then back up at the conductor, receiving feed-

back and guidance that influenced how they sang. In regular cycles, they would look down at their music to check the composition, then make eye contact with the conductor. At key moments in the song, singers would glance to check in with the members of their group within the choir or with a soloist who was about to sing.

This way, they got the cues they needed to achieve perfect harmony. The result was so extraordinary that Dan could feel the hair prickle on the back of his neck. After the choir had finished and left the stage—following a standing ovation that lasted a couple of minutes—he could still hear their beautiful singing in his head.

The next act was good, but not great like the choir. Dan found his thoughts drifting to all the work that had been involved in organizing the event. The nonprofit itself didn't have the same level of harmony as the choir, so it had been a tough process. Even producing the invitation had been a nightmare. The event committee had spent time putting together an invitation they believed would get people excited about the event. Then they e-mailed it to the development committee, who thought it should include more information about the work of the organization and encourage people to donate, not just buy tickets. So they rewrote it and sent it back.

The event committee members were confused and upset because they felt the invitation no longer struck the tone they wanted. They rewrote it again, taking out or rewording what the development people had put in, and then e-mailed it back. The development committee was still not happy, and the situation escalated over the course of a week, with growing frustration evident in the chain of e-mails. Finally, the problem ended up going all the way to the board.

Michael reminded the two committees that they were meant to be working toward the same shared goal, not moving in polar opposite directions. He got them to agree to stop their e-mail back-and-forth, sit down together in a room, look at the problem, and find common ground. They had a detailed discussion to figure out what should and should not be said in the invitation and were able to solve their differences in one discussion. They sent the invitation to the printers that afternoon.

Dan wished for a time when everyone in the nonprofit consistently worked together in greater harmony and had fewer situations like this. And then if everyone could just start performing more harmoniously at his workplace, things would really be looking up.

All too often, most of us feel like Dan, wishing that the organizations we interact with on a daily basis would get their act together and work more cohesively. It can be frustrating to deal with an organization where the members are out of sync with one another and with your needs. You can hear the discord, so why on earth can't they hear that the music they're playing isn't very pleasing?

At some time in your life—at a high school concert, for instance—you have probably found yourself wincing in the first few seconds when there is a discordant note or someone misses the beat. Maybe the musicians just need to settle down and find their groove, you might think at first—except it keeps happening. Meanwhile, up on stage the musicians continue as though nothing is wrong. They play intently, concentrating deeply on what they're doing.

Part of the reason groups keep playing as though they haven't noticed their own discord is that each musician probably thinks they are doing the right thing. They practiced their part of the composition, and they think they're performing it spot on. In a large band or orchestra, they probably additionally got together with the members of their section to rehearse. So as a section, they also think they're hitting the mark. But because everyone isn't working together as a whole unit, there are far too many sour notes.

The same thing frequently happens in organizations. One person or group does what they think is the right thing—only they don't realize how it will affect other parts of the organization.

Remember Dan's hospital visit, mentioned in chapter 2, when he was left waiting a long time for the doctor? What he didn't know was that the delay was actually the result of staff trying to improve his experience.

Administrators in hospitals frequently strive to improve performance, and one way they can show measurable improvement is by cutting the time patients spend sitting in the waiting room. Let's say a hospital makes its procedures more efficient, and as a result they can get a patient out of the waiting room and into the doctor's office in half the time it used to take. They are applauded for this efficiency.

However, the hospital still has the same number of doctors, and it still takes each doctor the same amount of time to process and treat a patient. So now, instead of sitting on a couch in the waiting room leafing through magazines, the patient spends ages perched on the edge of an exam table, shivering in a hospital gown, in a room that was designed for receiving medical treatment, not sitting comfortably.

The administrators genuinely believed they were doing the right thing. But if they were an orchestra, it would be as though they had just rewritten one part of the composition without thinking about the whole symphony. While perfecting the way one section performed, they were not looking at how all of the sections of the orchestra interact with one another to create a harmonious sound for the audience. Even when Individuals or certain groups within an organization are performing with excellence, if they're not playing well together as a whole, the quality of the organization's products or services suffer.

Forming Chords—The Core of Teamwork

In music, a chord is made up of three or more notes played at the same time. Chords are considered the building blocks of harmony. In an organization, a chord is made up of the actions performed by two or more people or groups of people at the same time. And just as is in music, the forming of chords is the basis for harmony within an organization.

Chord: The actions of two or more individuals or groups within an organization that together produce a harmonious outcome.

For a group of people to achieve a perfect chord, each individual needs to know the part they are meant to be playing, how it complements the rest of the group's efforts, and where it fits within the overall work of the organization. The composition—that is, the plan of the work—needs to be designed in such a way that when individuals perform their roles, everything comes together harmoniously to create the ideal outcome every time. People also need to know the tempo they are meant to follow, so that they are in step with everyone else in the organization and the customer. And they need a sense of how to work together as a team.

Breaking Down Silos

One of the most disruptive types of discord arises when departments within an organization operate as individual silos rather than working together toward a shared goal. Each group thinks it is doing the right thing, but they're actually at odds with one another.

The turmoil over the fundraiser invitation for Dan's nonprofit was a classic example of this. In fact, discord over the document approval process is familiar to most people who have worked in organizations. In nonprofits, for example, it may center around policy statements, grant applications, or fundraising letters. In business, it might be sales and marketing brochures, advertising copy, or training manuals. No matter the type of document or the type of organization, the document usually needs to be checked off by multiple departments that may each approach it with their own agenda.

The result is that departments that should be coordinating with one another can end up at odds with one another. One department does its work while another undoes that work and redoes it. And the first department undoes that work and redoes it, and so on. The same pattern occurs in many activities in an organization.

The cause is always the same: departmental silos that are focusing only on what they want to get done and their own priorities. And the solution is always the same: get everybody back on Absolute Pitch. Get them all on the same page and playing the same music.

Making Sure You Have the Right Teams

If you were to sit down for a concert by a world-class orchestra, you would assume that the musicians on stage had gone through a rigorous selection process, wouldn't you? Only those who are the most talented and the best suited to their roles would have been chosen for such an honor. Special care would have been given to bring together musicians who work well with the members of their section, the orchestra as a whole, and the conductor. You also would assume that a musician who had been giving substandard performances or not gelling with everyone else in their section would have been replaced if they didn't improve.

These facts are all self-evident. We know that these are some of the reasons a world-class orchestra is a world-class orchestra.

Similarly, an Absolute Pitch organization continually makes an effort to ensure it has the right people with the right skills working in the roles to which they are best suited.

If you were to look closely at the makeup of the teams in your organization, you might find that you would be better off with fewer people in some, or more people in others. You might discover that some people should really be moved to different roles or different teams. The key takeaway here is not whether you need to cut or change personnel; it's that any organization striving for Absolute Pitch should be regularly assessing its people, their roles, and how they work together. Building this process into the way your organization operates is what's important.

Yet organizations often avoid this process. Some fear that while they are taking time out to address whether they have the right people in the right roles, their competitors will overtake them in the marketplace. Others are concerned about negative reactions if the process uncovers that some people's roles need to be phased out or they need to be replaced. Personal relationships and office politics can also come into play. So rather than making decisions about whether the right people are in the right roles, they simply continue making do with what they've got.

The costs of avoiding this process are high. Let's imagine what this would look like in our orchestra example: Say that the principal violinist keeps skipping rehearsals and is clashing with several of the other violinists. Meanwhile, over in the woodwind section a brilliant flute player is filling in on piccolo though he's mediocre at it. One percussionist, whose real passion is to play in a rock band, needs to be nudged all the time by the others to remember to play her part. What happens if the directors of the orchestra don't do anything about these causes of disharmony? Problems start to creep in. Someone doesn't hit the right note. One musician is out of sync with the others in their section. Someone is off the beat. There are moments when everyone is no longer following the conductor perfectly. They stop getting standing ovations, and their "world-class" status slips.

It can sometimes be tough to make decisions about personnel, but an Absolute Pitch organization realizes that they're better off taking the time to make sure they have the equivalent of the right musicians in the right chairs, playing their parts at the right time, following the right composition. They pause, slow down, look carefully at what they're trying to deliver to the customer. They ensure they have the right people to make it possible.

Leading the Organization to Harmony

Even with the right people in the right roles, harmony doesn't just happen by itself. It requires consistently good leadership at every level of the organization.

In an orchestra, it begins with having a maestro as a conductor who sets the right tempo and mood for everyone as a group. It also hinges on the leaders of each section of the orchestra. When those of us who aren't symphony fans look at the string section, we may perceive little distinction between individual violin players—we may simply see twenty musicians all dressed in black, their bows going back and forth at the same time. In fact, they are split into two distinct groups (first and second violins). The individuals in each of those groups seek direction not only from the conductor but also from the leader of their group. This person is known as "first chair" because they sit closest to the conductor. While the violinists keep their eye on the conductor, they also take cues from the first chair, watching for the movement of their bow.

It's easy to see that if the conductor or the first chair starts behaving in a different way—the conductor quickens the pace with her baton or the first chair violinist comes in early on his part—everyone else will follow their lead. Inevitably, this will change the way the music sounds.

The same is true for all organizations: the way the leaders act influences how everyone behaves. This applies to all leaders, ranging from people who lead small teams within the organization up to the president or CEO. It's not so much the words said but the behavior that others will follow. If leaders act in harmony with the rest of the organization and its values, they begin to create a harmonious environment. But when they set aside the sheet music everyone was following and act in a different way, they introduce discord.

The challenge for leadership is to be consistent in modeling the right behavior. When faced with urgent deadlines, budget problems, or other pressures, it is all too easy to set aside the organization's values and instead find the most expedient solution. It's the equivalent of a commanding officer in the heat of battle ripping up the plans and rashly leading a charge at the enemy.

When faced with a crisis, stepping on the gas is the easiest option—and in the short term, it gets the job done. However, it can have negative impacts on the organization in the medium or long term. For instance, perhaps quality declines, which hurts the company in the marketplace down the track. People within the organization may be exhausted and burnt out, no longer giving their best, or they may leave the organization entirely.

When challenges arise, leaders in Absolute Pitch organizations act consistently and in a way that they know benefits the organization. They think things through to find a long-term solution.

Coordinating Teams

In a symphony, every section of the orchestra has its time to shine. You may barely be aware of the percussionists—until the music gradually swells, building to a crescendo of thundering drums and crashing cymbals. It sounds wonderful to your ears because they played their part at the right time in the composition, taking their cue from the conductor and the other musicians. But if they had come in booming and crashing too early —say, during a flute solo—they would have thrown the performance into disharmony.

In the same way, for an organization to achieve Absolute Pitch, its teams need to be coordinated perfectly so that the emphasis falls on the work of the correct team at the correct moment. For instance, when Michael's technology company plans to launch a new consumer product, multiple teams within and outside of the company are involved: engineers and researchers in the product development division, the manufacturing supply chain, packaging design and manufacture, and marketing and sales.

The work of all of these teams has to come together perfectly so that the product is ready to hit the marketplace exactly on the optimal date. To succeed, each group needs to make its contribution to the highest possible standard and on time. Clearly, this will require a tremendous amount of coordination among all groups. As is the case in any organization, they will need to work in concert with one another.

At a given time in an organization, there may be one particular team that needs to stand up and take the lead position. If Michael's company decides on further expansion in the future, the procurement department will need to find larger global suppliers. Similarly, if the nonprofit he and Dan volunteer for gets a new big donor who increases the volume of food in their warehouse, the volunteer department will need to do a recruitment drive before the team who handles distribution can take center stage.

In some instances, the groups in an organization are called upon to play their parts in a specific sequence. It's like when you're at a big Fourth of July event and the band plays a patriotic medley; they might start out with part of "The Star-Spangled Banner," then shift to several verses of "America the Beautiful," followed by "The Stars and Stripes Forever." To create harmony, all of the members in the band need to get the sequence right and wait for each song to be completed before starting the next.

It may sound like a no-brainer that a band has to get this right. But many organizations are also called upon to play medleys and often get the sequence wrong.

Medley: A sequence of three or more teams' outcomes that together lead to a bigger overall outcome.

Going back to the example of Michael's technology company, the ultimate aim of the business is to deliver its products to retailers and receive payment. Stage 1 of the medley would be that the sales team secures an order for the product. Once stage 2 is complete, the manufacturing division does its part and produces it. When the product is ready, the finance department begins stage 3 of the medley, invoicing, and the shipping department then initiates stage 4, which is the delivery of the product to the retailers.

Each team that carries out one of these stages is working

toward its own outcome, but each team's outcome needs to be timed and sequenced correctly with the other teams' if they are going to succeed at reaching the overall outcome they are aiming for as a company. The overall outcome is the sum of all the teams' outcomes.

Listening for Sour Notes

If a band strikes a discordant note at the start of a song, they can get back on track if they react quickly and make a correction. On the other hand, if they don't recognize their mistake and just keep playing, the sour notes can multiply until the song finally ends—to the great relief of the audience.

In organizations, it's just as crucial to recognize sour notes and correct them as soon as possible. Naturally, leadership needs to be tuned in at all times and stay abreast of what is happening. In the context of an orchestra, we could say that the first chairs of each section need to be checking in with the musicians in their sections. For instance, they may pick up on discord during rehearsal time and then talk with the conductor and with the principals of other sections.

An Absolute Pitch organization creates an environment in which everyone, not only those in leadership positions, listens for sour notes and speaks up when they hear one instead of just continuing to play their part as though nothing has happened.

Essentially, in an Absolute Pitch organization, listening out for minor discord is a part of how everyone does their work. The message is driven home to every individual that being alert to missteps is a part of the organization's mission and is everyone's responsibility.

If you make listening out for discord a systemic part of your organization's processes, you will find that you can respond to sour notes much more quickly. You will be able to take corrective action faster and more easily—and you will be a step closer to Absolute Pitch.

~

A Wake-Up Call for Dan

Spending an afternoon fishing with Michael weeks before had freed Dan of distractions and taken him out of his everyday life for a few hours, giving him perspective and a chance to think. With a clearer focus, the following Monday he had gone in to work and brought all the relevant parties together and resolved the situation that had been bugging him: by finding a common purpose, all had come to an agreement that big soft couches weren't a great idea on the factory floor. They chose instead to set some limits on working hours so the personnel weren't exhausted. They were to spend time recharging their batteries or being with their families. That way, they would have the ability to do work they could be proud of and deliver the highest standard of quality.

Since then, Dan had been repeating this to the manager like a mantra. The manager, in turn, had been repeating it to the personnel on the factory floor.

Realizing that a short break from his everyday concerns had helped him think more clearly that day, Dan now got up early to ride a stationary bike at the gym most mornings. Today he'd invited Michael along for their Absolute Pitch catch-up. Michael had just finished recapping the keys to creating harmony in an organization. Dan had been listening quietly, and even when Michael had finished, he stayed silent.

"Something on your mind?" Michael asked.

"Well, it occurred to me while you were talking that even though the manager and I have been giving clear instructions to the guys on the factory floor not to work every minute of the day and rush through jobs in a crisis, things are pretty much the same," said Dan. "I haven't seen a noticeable change in behavior."

"Hmm, so let me tell you about something I learned the hard way that might help you out," replied Michael. He recounted that when

his business was young, he was launching a complex innovative tech-nology. There was a plan in place that would take five years to execute, and success would depend on several teams each hitting multiple deadlines along the way. From the company's beginning, Michael had set up a clear mission and values. "It wasn't all that much different from the mantra you've been giving your guys," he told Dan.

One of the teams of engineers had a looming deadline to produce a prototype of one of the components. Because of delays in getting the data and the materials they needed, they were running a couple of weeks behind schedule. However, the head of the division only found out at the last minute because no one passed the word up to her.

"When word finally made its way to me, I communicated in no uncertain terms that it was imperative they make the deadline," said Michael. "You know I'm from an engineering background, so I rolled up my sleeves and got stuck into the job that needed to be done.

"The head of the division and the lead engineer started working alongside me all day and all night to get it done. The whole team followed suit," Michael continued. "We each put in more than 100 hours of work during the week. The only time I saw my wife and kids was as I walked in the door for a couple hours' sleep and a shower.

"We finished in time, and I was so proud of myself and the team. But after that wore off, I thought about it in a new light. We'd inevitably had to take shortcuts, telling ourselves that we would get it right in the next version of the prototype. And there I was, touting a mission that was all about quality and excellence and family time.

"I was telling people to perform one way while I was behaving in the opposite way. And I sure as heck wasn't creating harmony," Michael said, shaking his head. "Until that moment, I'd always thought of disharmony as just something that I needed to fix in other people."

Dan's legs felt heavy as he pedaled—and it wasn't only because they were nearing the end of their ride. He thought about all the times he'd burned the midnight oil or sanctioned his staff to do so. Then he tried to think of what other choice he had in the circumstances, and he came up blank. With a querying look on his face, he turned to Michael, who was already a step ahead of him.

"In an Absolute Pitch organization, leaders do their best to act according to the organization's values and the plan everyone is following. They stay on message. Whenever someone else is acting against the organization's values or the plan, they intervene," said Michael. "So when something like that happened again, I called a time-out. I said to my department heads, 'Wait a second, we're off tempo. We're moving too fast, and we're asking too much of our people.'"

"And then what did you do?"

"Then we looked at the underlying causes. We worked to find the root of our issues," said Michael. "If you're going to get encore performances, that's what you're going to have to do."

5

SETTING THE TEMPO AND CREATING THE MELODY

F rom an office with a floor-to-ceiling window, Dan and Michael looked down on a factory floor where one of Michael's products was being assembled. Staff went about their tasks with focus and precision; at key stages along the line, green indicator lights showed that everything was running smoothly. Dan was impressed with just how much thought and planning had gone into the design of the space. He was glad Michael had brought him here to see it.

"Green is good!" said Michael.

"Indeed it is," replied Dan, whose company used the same indicator system at its manufacturing facilities.

"Ah, I spoke too soon," Michael said as one of the lights turned to amber, indicating that there was a problem brewing. A supervisor came over to check on the equipment and speak to the operator. "You can't completely avoid problems arising—obviously!" Michael commented with a grin. "What truly matters is what happens next: Do you respond in a timely way? Do you work out what you need to do to get back on track? Or do you just keep plodding on, hoping that the amber light won't turn red?"

Dan winced inside. Lately he had seen too many red lights indicating that work had come to a halt. "To me, those red lights signal lost opportunities to win customers in the new markets we're planning to launch in," he said. "You know how you were talking about tempo a while back? Well, every red light I see now, I think about how it puts us one step further behind the tempo our potential customers would like us to be moving at."

"Obviously, we all need to make our customers happy," replied Michael, "but are you sure that it's the customer's *tempo you need to be timing your work to?"*

"Hmm." Dan stopped and cast his mind back to his previous conversations with Michael. What piece of the puzzle was he forgetting? "The consumer," he said finally. Then he thought some more. "But wait, in my business, isn't the person who truly matters the one who writes the check? If we're late delivering a new imaging device, our account manager has to deal with a disgruntled hospital administrator, not a technician in scrubs. Surely I have to get everyone

working at a tempo that meets the administrator's expectations, don't I?"

"It might seem so," said Michael, "but let's peel a layer off the onion, okay? Years ago, we put out a great productivity software product—or so we thought. The product was far ahead of everything else on the market and very attractive to our big corporate customers.

"The thing was, their staff wasn't ready to use the technology. The rest of their systems were a couple of years behind, so they couldn't integrate our innovations. The software ended up unused. Sales dropped off sharply. Ever since then, we've done more research on our consumers and the pace they want us to move at."

It was not a part of Dan's company's practice to find out the opinions of the medical staff who operated their equipment or the doctors who ordered tests and treatments. But now it occurred to Dan that unless they built that practice into their operations, their customers might be left holding on to underutilized, high-cost devices—and they just might turn to competitors who were keeping up with their tempo.

For a group of musicians to receive a standing ovation, they have to perform at a tempo that's pleasing to the audience. And as Dan has just learned, for an organization to achieve Absolute Pitch, it needs to provide its products or services at the pace set by its consumers. In chapter 2, we talked about why it's important for an organization to think carefully about tempo before they begin their work. Now let's look at the practicalities of setting the tempo, maintaining it, and adapting to changing conditions and level of demand.

Counting the Beat

When a composer writes a piece of music, the meter they choose determines the beat of the music. In everyday terms, this is the beat you find yourself tapping your foot or clapping along to.

The beat at which an organization moves is determined by the amount of work that is completed in a certain amount of time.

Meter: The units of work completed in a set time period.

For example, in the factory that Dan just visited with Michael, it may take a worker one minute to perform a task on the product they're assembling. Working at a steady pace, if there are 100 products for that worker to perform the task on, it will take them 100 minutes. The meter is one task per minute, and the composer can plan the work based upon that meter.

Now imagine what happens if the worker who is usually at that station on the production line has to do jury duty and someone less experienced fills in for a week. This new person can handle only one product every two minutes.

The composition—the plan the organization is trying to work to—required an output of one task per minute. But now the performance is under way, and the pace of the actual work is different. The symphony no longer sounds the way the composer intended it.

Understanding the Role of the Conductor

It is almost impossible for the work of any group to perfectly match the tempo set by the composition, because circumstances always arise that force people off their plan. For a group to excel, it needs a conductor who makes continual adjustments so that the symphony still sounds amazing to the audience.

Yet the majority of organizations fail to either recognize or adapt when circumstances push them off their composition. They don't change their expectations of the output. Nor do they make changes to enable people to return to the planned pace of work and meet the original expectations.

In an Absolute Pitch organization, on the other hand, the conductor is aware of a problem as soon as it arises and makes changes to get everyone back to the composition. There are many ways this could be achieved. For instance, in Michael's factory, the conductor might call a rehearsal—that is, a supervisor might get a more experienced worker to pause what they're doing to help the new person get up to speed.

Carrying a Strong Melody

What can you do to give your organization the best chance of quickly adapting to changed circumstances and getting back to your composition? It all comes down to fostering the right patterns of behavior.

Another way to look at this is to imagine what you'd need to do if you were all singing together. To give a great performance, you would need to carry a strong melody, wouldn't you? In a song, the melody is the progression of notes that together make up the tune you sing or hum along to. The notes in a melody form a pattern that is repeatable. Without that pattern, you don't have a catchy tune.

While the composition represents the ideal of how the organization's planned work will be performed, the melody is people's actual behavior as they attempt to follow that plan.

Melody: The pattern of behavior of individuals that forms the organization's output

---

Let's say Michael's business begins the year with a revenue forecast, and they formulate a plan to achieve those numbers. But as soon as work begins, there are countless factors each day that knock people off the plan. There might be a problem with a supplier, bad weather could interrupt shipping, a computer network might go down, and so on. To get back on track, they will need to make adjustments. It is much easier to make those adjustments if they have established the right patterns of behavior to begin with.

In an Absolute Pitch organization like Michael's, people truly understand how their individual work contributes to the whole organization. They know that for the symphony to sound great, they have to play their music well. This knowledge gives them a compelling reason to behave the right way—that is, to behave in the way that benefits the whole organization. When factors push them off their composition, they notice that their music doesn't sound the way it should. They stand up and say, "We need a rehearsal."

This means that melody is tied closely to a concept we looked at in chapter 2: the importance of setting criteria by which to make choices that benefit the whole organization rather than just the individual. To have the right pattern of behavior—that is, the right melody—individuals need the correct composition to follow. Otherwise, they may make bad choices. They might fail to consider the organization as a whole and slow their tempo down because that is easier for them as individuals. Or in a crisis, they might focus on their own short-term gain: they might jump in as the rock star and speed up the tempo rather than involving other team members to come up with a long-term solution to the underlying problem.

Taking the Organization's Pulse

Of course, for a conductor to make an adjustment, they first need to be aware that one is needed. In an orchestra, it might be relatively easy for a conductor standing in front of the musicians on the stage to hear when something goes wrong. In an organization, especially a large one, it can be significantly more challenging.

So how does the conductor in an organization know when an individual or a group has departed from the plan?

If you ever took music lessons, you will be familiar with the metronome, which ticks at a set number of beats per minute so that you can learn to play a piece of music at a steady tempo. The metronome's ticking is like the heartbeat of the music. It's the music's pulse. Every organization also has a pulse, and an Absolute Pitch organization sets up management systems to monitor it. That way, they always know whether they are hitting the correct tempo, playing the right melody, and striking the perfect chords to achieve the symphonic result they're working toward.

Pulse-taking: A management system that monitors the "heartbeat" of the organization to check whether it is achieving the right tempo, melody, and chords to produce the desired outcome.

During a symphony performance, the conductor's role is partly to keep everyone on the beat, but they are more than just a human metronome. The conductor is continually listening to the musicians and guiding them to make minor changes to the quality of their playing—for instance, louder or quieter, with greater or less intensity—in order to produce the desired effect on the audience. They don't wait for the critics' reviews the next day to see how the orchestra is performing; they monitor what is happening moment by moment and use that information to shape the performance in real time.

In a similar way, an Absolute Pitch organization sets up management systems that take the pulse of the organization and alert the right people when the performance has strayed from the composition.

Designing a System to Take the Pulse

The fundamental question an organization needs to answer when designing a management system for taking the pulse is: "Who needs to know what, when?"

Which personnel need a status update and how often they need one varies from organization to organization or from project to project. So your organization should tailor a system to your unique requirements. It needs to be based on how often you need to take the pulse in order to judge whether you're sticking to your plan and who needs to know.

Circumstances are continually changing, which means that the answer to the question "Who needs to know what, when?" can also change. Many organizations discovered this during the financial crisis of 2007. They had to rapidly adapt to changing market conditions if they were to survive. The organizations that stood the best chance of navigating the rough waters recognized that the traditional end-of-month report from their accounting department was no longer enough. They called for more reports more often, because they knew they had to take the organization's pulse more frequently than before.

It is similarly important for organizations to recognize when conditions are stable and things are running smoothly and design the pulse-taking process to suit those circumstances. When people in an organization report more frequently or in greater detail than is needed, productivity suffers.

Responding to Warning Signals

Warning signals such as yellow or red in the "traffic light" system that Dan and Michael were familiar with indicate when work is not going according to plan. What they don't show is how people got off the plan or how to get them back on it.

It's like when you're driving down the highway and all of a sudden your "check engine" light flashes. You could keep driving and hope that you will make it to your destination, but it's a much better idea to pull over and have someone check under the hood to find out what's wrong.

Responding too quickly to a warning signal can be as much of a problem as responding too slowly though. You do need to get back on the plan, but first you need to find out how you got off the plan to begin with. Otherwise it will happen again in the future. When an Absolute Pitch organization gets a warning signal, they take time to diagnose what is going on: At what stage in the process did the tempo go wrong? Is there discord in the organization that needs to be addressed? Is everyone in unison?

Just as an orchestra gets together to rehearse in order to fix sour notes in their performance, an organization should regularly spend time assessing where their performance is falling short and how to improve. In the next chapter, we're going to talk about out how your organization can use rehearsals to do exactly that.

~

Dan Asks "Who Needs to Know What, When?"

Watching the way the supervisor at Michael's factory had quickly responded to an amber signal got Dan thinking. First it jolted him into admitting that his company's factories weren't doing the best job of responding to their own amber signals in order to fix minor issues before they turned into big problems. Clearly, that was something they would have to address.

Dan's idea had expanded beyond that though. Everyone in their factories was used to the "traffic light" system. They knew they needed continual status updates because it was a serious problem if production ground to a halt. Essentially, the traffic light system told supervisors what they needed to know, when they needed to know it.

Now, thought Dan, it was time the rest of the organization had reporting systems that were as effective.

The company had set a target date for launching into the new markets for which they had gained regulatory approval. But it had passed . . . a couple of times. Dan was now able to identify one of their problems: they had not designed a system at the outset to ensure the right people had the right progress updates at the right time.

They had been relying on their customary way of taking the organization's pulse. Every month they would get everyone together for a meeting that ran half a day. Key staff from each division were each allocated time to report on their progress, complete with written reports and detailed PowerPoint presentations. Staff would stay late for days in the lead-up to the meeting, perfecting their presentations.

Since it became clear at one of the monthly meetings that they weren't going to make their projected launch date, everyone had been scrambling to go faster, work longer, and do whatever they needed to get ready to launch.

If they continued on with that approach, they would get to the finish line eventually. But Dan knew that if they started taking steps now to improve the way they took the company's pulse, the rest of the project would go more smoothly and lead to a better outcome.

If they didn't start developing a better approach now, they would likely find themselves in this unenviable position again the next time they tackled a major project.

Dan began to formulate some strategies for how they could take the pulse more often and in a less time-consuming way. Instead of waiting for a whole month to go by, they could have a progress update every other week. Rather than relying on long reports and PowerPoint presentations, they could create a better plan for who reported to whom. Information would flow in a timely manner from the people who were working closely on the project up to the relevant decision-makers at higher levels.

For instance, to stay on track, the manager of one of their factories might need frequent updates from the supervisors in order to make daily adjustments to the plan or the way work was being performed. On the other hand, a senior VP wouldn't need continual updates on the workings of the factory but would need to be alerted in a timely manner to any significant issues that arose.

Once he had thought it through, Dan would share his ideas about pulse-taking with his colleagues. It was the first time he had felt excited at work for years.

6

REHEARSING FOR PERFECTION

Dan had heard about the perks of working at some of the top technology companies, like free massages, foosball tables, and not having to pick up dry cleaning ever again. He thought these were just legends, like tales about unicorns. But as he was being shown through a tech company run by one of Michael's friends, Ava, he had to reassess his beliefs.

"I've never seen a workplace like this," he muttered under his breath to Michael as they walked through an expansive work area.

Few walls separated workstations, and those walls were made of glass. There were no doors to be seen. Natural light filled the room, and from every desk there was a view of a lake and tall trees. "What's this? It looks like a space capsule—admittedly a very nice space capsule," Dan said, pointing at a round white structure. There were several of them dotted around the space.

"It's a soundproof meeting pod," Ava answered. As they walked by, Michael looked in to see three people sitting inside having a discussion. "We've put them strategically throughout the space so that when people need to work through something with their team, they can pop in and talk without disturbing anyone."

They passed through the workspace into the break room. "Just wait till you taste the food," Michael said. From the corner of his eye, Dan had indeed registered the buffet table running along one wall. It offered a bounty of fresh fruit, baked goods, and gourmet treats. But the true focus of his attention was the two swings hanging from the ceiling in the far corner of the room. The swings were currently in use, and the people using them were oblivious to Dan's gaze because they were intently talking about something.

All around the room people sat and chatted, had coffee together, grabbed a healthy snack. The atmosphere was serene but energized.

Dan and Michael selected some food from the buffet and then sat down in chairs that were arranged in a circle around a coffee table. As Ava made a fresh pot of coffee at a station near the buffet, Michael turned to Dan and said, "So, you see why I brought you here?"

Actually, Dan had been so busy taking in the scene around him that he hadn't got to wondering about that yet. "Now that you mention it, why are we here?" he answered.

"We're here because this place clearly illustrates one of the most important principles of Absolute Pitch," Michael said.

"Oh great," said Dan. "Wait, what is it?"

"Actually, you've already seen it during our walk-through."

Dan craned his neck to see what he'd missed. "The best I can come up with is: they look after their employees really well so they retain the best talent," he offered.

"Yes, that's true," said Michael. "But that's not it."

"They provide everything that anybody could ever need so they don't have to leave the building during the workday. It makes them more productive," Dan tried next.

Ava had just joined them and put the tray of coffees down. Michael said, "Thanks, Ava. Now help him out here."

"See all that food there on the buffet and see these chairs we're sitting in?" she said as she made herself comfortable opposite Dan. "It's not just food, and these aren't just pieces of furniture."

Dan looked at her blankly. Then he cast his gaze from her to Michael as steam curled up from their mugs on the low table in front of them. He smiled. "This is all about bringing people together," he said.

"That's right. It's about getting conversations started and getting ideas flowing. Some of our most successful business innovations were born from discussions that started right here," said Ava. "And by making it easy for people to come together, our teams are more likely to deal with issues before they become problems."

"It might not look like it, but this is one of the ways that people in this company rehearse," added Michael. "Sure, it might not be the right rehearsal approach for every organization. But every organization certainly does need to find its own version of rehearsal if they're going to aim for Absolute Pitch."

∽

When we see exceptional musicians on stage, it can seem as though they must have been born with a magical gift, an innate talent that enables them to effortlessly give a mind-blowing performance. It's easy to overlook all of the many hours of hard work that went into the hour or so of entertainment we're enjoying.

In fact, what happens on stage is just a fraction of musicians' work. Take people who earn their living in a professional orchestra: They spend hours each day practicing their instruments. They listen to recordings or familiarize themselves with the composition they're going to perform. Then they practice their parts on their own, over and over. And in the week leading up to a concert, they rehearse with the whole orchestra, adjusting their performances to the conductor's unifying vision.

Similarly, for any exceptional organization, their delivery of top-notch products or services is just part of what they do. They take regular time-outs away from their day-to-day work so they can reexamine the composition and the way they are playing their parts. They use this time to get better at what they do. The result is that they consistently wow their audience when they are performing.

Rehearsal: The time individuals spend practicing the behaviors that lead to Absolute Pitch.

People in most organizations spend little time planning, preparing, or practicing. This is because they are not measured or rewarded for doing so, or the environment doesn't give them the opportunity. Absolute Pitch organizations, on the other hand, factor in time for their people to review performance and find ways to improve. They provide individuals with forums in which to come together and discuss what's working and what's not and how to improve. They measure and reward teams not only for performance but also for getting together to rehearse.

Rehearsal can take many forms, depending on the unique situation of each organization. Some build rehearsal time into their schedules through regular conferences and meetings. Some have formal training, development, and education programs. Others, like Ava's company, focus on designing an environment that encourages people to get together for discussions as a natural part of daily work.

No matter what form rehearsals take in an Absolute Pitch organization, the intent is the same: to turn planning, preparation, and practice into routine elements of how the organization operates. Rehearsal is part of the leadership's ethos, and it is integral to the organization as a whole. The leadership sets clear, attainable goals for those rehearsals.

An important goal of rehearsal is behavioral improvement. Imagine that your organization has recently gone through the process of establishing its values. As we saw in chapter 2, these values will now determine the decisions that individuals in your organization make every day. If people are presented with a choice—they can do A or they can do B—they need to make the choice that is aligned with your organization's values. They need to make that choice every time. But as anyone who has ever tried to change a habit knows, it can take a lot of practice to reach the point where you automatically make the correct choice each time. That is why rehearsals are so important: they give everyone the opportunity to practice the behavior expected of them.

Building Effective Teams—The Core of Rehearsal

You might be surprised to hear how many times a professional orchestra rehearses together before a performance. Despite the complexity of a symphony, they usually need to rehearse as a whole orchestra only about four times before the concert. The reason they can attain a high standard of excellence in a handful of sessions is that they come to rehearsal fully prepared. They practice their instruments regularly; they have practiced their parts; and if the piece of music is especially challenging, they have come together with the rest of their section to practice. They arrive prepared to give their best.

Similarly, if members of an organization spend time practicing within their teams, it is easier for the organization to perform as a whole and be more productive, efficient, and effective. This is because in rehearsal the members of the team get together to script their interactions with one other and also with the greater organization. They discuss the choices they are presented with each day, and they learn which choices align with the organization's values and lead to the overall desired outcome. They discover how their contributions fit into the team's efforts and the organization's efforts as a whole.

Because team rehearsals give people a chance to learn how to improve the way they behave, they can, in turn, help to change the culture of the whole organization. For instance, organizational silos (see chapter 4) may seem like an overwhelming problem to tackle, but rehearsing with your own team gives you a place to start. In your practice sessions, your team members can start to change their behavior so that they are working in harmony with the rest of the team and with other teams. If your team keeps practicing that behavior, you will be modeling it to everyone else in your organization. Before long, your influence will have spread through the whole organization, and other people will set a goal to work harmoniously too.

Using Rehearsals to Improve Your Stage Setting

When an orchestra walks out on stage, the musicians don't just grab any seat and sit down. Each section has its own place, and each musician has a particular position within the section as well. Everyone is arranged on the stage in a way that is optimal for the conductor and the musicians to see and hear one another and to make the best of the room's acoustics.

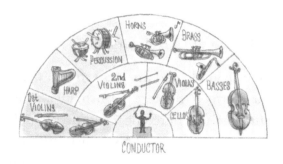

In many organizations, however, the way the "stage" is set up has not been optimally designed for people to interact with one another or carry out their tasks. Rehearsal time can be used to find ways to improve the ergonomics to make their workflow more efficient.

This can be a valuable step no matter the size or complexity of the organization. At the scale of an international business such as Michael's, for instance, an order might have to pass through the hands of multiple people in multiple countries and time zones to be fulfilled. For Dan, a component of one of their medical devices might need to travel from a factory in one state to a factory on the other side of the country for assembly. At the factories, each machinist's ergonomics need to be considered: Is their equipment easy to reach? How many times do they have to turn their body? Do they have to make any unnecessary movements?

Like all organizations, these companies have a choice: they can simply continue to do the work the way they've always worked or they can take a moment to pause and look at the ergonomics of how the work is done. Rehearsal gives them the chance to design the way work is performed to make if flow better, more harmoniously, and more efficiently.

Boosting Resilience with Rehearsals

No matter how accomplished an orchestra is, there can be no such thing as a "perfect" concert performance. Any number of things can influence the outcome in unpredictable ways—an audience member sneezes, a percussionist comes in a fraction of a second too soon, a string breaks on the guest soloist's violin.

No organization will ever be able to follow its plan perfectly either, because we all have to face changing circumstances. Everything from a personnel shortage to a sudden jolt in economic conditions or a delay in the delivery of supplies due to a hurricane may mean that we simply cannot do what we planned. Or perhaps the level of consumer demand rises or falls, and the tempo you planned to work at is now too slow or too fast.

Too many organizations put their heads down and try to

ignore the real world as it intrudes on their ideal plan. In the worst-case scenario, this can even spell the demise of an organization. Yet some organizations stand out from the rest by showing resilience in the face of changing or imperfect circumstances. They pause, acknowledge that the situation is not what they planned for, and adapt without delay.

The reason some organizations are better at adapting is because they have spent time regularly rehearsing. As a result, the individuals are in sync with the members of their team and with the rest of the organization; their performance flows far more fluidly than if they hadn't rehearsed. In addition, they have had the chance to develop a greater repertoire of strategies to deal with contingencies.

In a well-rehearsed orchestra, if the guest soloist's violin string breaks, the players rapidly respond—the first violinist may quickly swap violins, allowing the solo to continue, while the violin is restrung offstage.

A similar example that is familiar to many people is football. Because it's such a strategic game, football teams rehearse their sets of plays over and over. They also take time to consider the variety of ways in which the defense might behave, and they rehearse how they will react. Of course, in the heat of the game things never go exactly according to plan. Even the very best team cannot predict every scenario. But the team that has practiced the most effectively reacts the most effectively. They might even turn the situation to their advantage.

So the question your organization needs to ask itself is not how to make your plan immune to changing circumstances; the real question is: have you rehearsed enough to be able to adapt to change so that to the outside world your work appears seamless, like an unstoppable football team in the middle of a play?

Improving by Improvising

When we think about improvisation in the music world, the image that springs to mind for most of us is a jazz ensemble noodling away late at night in a dimly lit club. So you might be surprised to hear that classical music greats such as Mozart, Bach, and Beethoven were adept at improvising when they performed their works. They embraced improvisation because they knew it could be fertile ground for fresh new ideas and improvements to the composition. Improvisation is also a valuable element of an Absolute Pitch organization's rehearsals.

Improvisation: A pause in an organization's performance, creating an environment for discovery in which individuals or teams can safely try out new approaches to their work.

Although improvisation can seem unplanned and even anarchic, it has rules and structure. For instance, while the saxophone player is making up a melody on the spot, beneath his melody chords are being played by the piano and double bass. Those chords follow a known and accepted progression that is pleasing to the ear. If the band threw away the chords, which are the bedrock of their harmony, the result would be chaotic noise.

In the same way, improvisation in an organization must be structured and consciously built into its processes. It also needs to have a clear goal—such as a dry run of a new method of doing something or a way to discover the roles to which people are best suited. If it doesn't have a clear goal, it's not really improvisation—it's an impromptu performance.

Impromptu performance: Work performed without a plan or with disregard for the plan.

The clearest example of an impromptu performance is that of the organization's "rock star," who rushes in to save the day when something has gone wrong.

The rock star deals with a crisis by setting aside the composition and doing something different.

In Dan's company, the delays in launching into new markets had led to a shortfall in projected revenue. To make the financials look okay, the CFO had made a snap decision to bring forward the fulfillment of future orders, regardless of when the customers wanted their equipment delivered. At the end of the month, when the financials were compiled, the CFO was seen as a savior; his impromptu performance sounded great to everyone's ears.

Unfortunately, though, that performance would not be repeatable. When people rehearse, they practice behavior so that they become good at it and can repeat it in the future at a consistently high standard. But when they act in an impromptu way, they're not practicing, which means they are unlikely to be able to give the same performance next time. In Dan's company, the only thing that is repeatable is that at the same time next month, they will face the same problem with the financials again.

In fact, the CFO's impromptu performance pushed the company even further away from their plan. It would take weeks to get back to the composition they were following previously, and the launch date seemed even more distant. His actions may have provided a quick fix, but they did not help the organization in the long term—in fact, they made things worse.

To come up with lasting solutions to problems or better ways to undertake work, an organization needs rehearsals. These may include planned improvisation sessions. Improvisation is desirable because it is part of the organization's processes. Impromptu performances are undesirable because they are not a part of the processes, and they steer the organization further away from Absolute Pitch.

Rehearsing Is Important for the Conductor

When an orchestra rehearses, the conductor is rehearsing too —practicing his or her interactions with the musicians, testing out different approaches, tailoring the style in which the composition will be performed. The conductor has their own vision for how the composition should be interpreted but will also take into consideration the input of all the sections of the orchestra.

In a well-run organization, leadership has an ongoing dialogue with the groups that make up the organization, and the groups' input informs the leadership's decision-making. This is one of the reasons it's important for leaders to build rehearsal time into their processes. A rehearsal gives leadership an opportunity to adjust the tempo, melody, and dynamics of the performance.

In music, "dynamics" refers to variations in the loudness of the notes—the quiet, gentle sections of a symphony; the loud, clamorous parts; and the crescendos that build and then subside. In an organization, "dynamics" refers to the variations in intensity that leadership brings to the way work is performed.

Dynamics: Changes in the intensity of the work performed in an organization.

A good example of this is the different interpretation that the leadership teams at Dan's company and Michael's company should be giving to their compositions. As Dan had realized, their methods for taking the pulse in relation to the launch weren't the most appropriate. Given the company's revenue shortfall, leadership also needed to rethink their financial pulse-taking. People's behavior also needed to change at Dan's company. Anyone who has ever lived through tough times or has saved up to buy something knows that the only way to succeed is to watch every penny. Until the company can come out the other side of this challenging period, people at Dan's company would need to be as efficient as possible by taking extra care with every single action.

Leadership sets the tone for the behaviors of people in the organization. If leadership at Dan's company took time for rehearsals to listen to what was going on in the organization, they would sense that it was time to change the melody they were playing. They would have an opportunity to intervene and refine the composition. Instead, they were allowing the performance to continue on unchanged. The longer this went on, the more problems were created.

Michael's company was in a better place financially, so they were in a position to behave differently in relation to money. They could worry less about every penny and make more strategic decisions with a long-term investment outlook. It had not always been smooth sailing at Michael's company though. Like any business, they had faced challenging times. But because of their commitment to regular rehearsal, their leadership had been able to recognize when the intensity needed to change—for instance, going back to once-a-month financial reporting rather than once-a-week during difficult times. They were also able to recognize when it was time for people in the organization to adopt behavior that was in line with a more long-term outlook. This switch in intensity had helped the company to grow.

∾

Michael Shares His Rehearsal and Improvement Story

There were only a couple of other people left in the break room now, and Ava had gone to a meeting. Dan looked out over the lake, which was starting to take on a golden hue as the sun sank low in the sky.

"I really do see your point about practice," said Dan. "But quite honestly, I'm just not sure how I'm going to convince other people at work that there's enough time in the day to schedule rehearsals on top of all the things they have to do, especially when we're already running behind on our launch."

"Here's another way for you to frame it," Michael replied. "Imagine if you were musicians in an orchestra and you didn't make time for practicing. When you got onstage, what would happen? You

would fall all over one another trying to sort out who sits where. You'd fumble around with your instruments. You'd flip through the sheet music trying to find your places."

"We'd hit more than a few bad notes," Dan added.

"Right. And reaching Absolute Pitch would seem almost impossible starting from there."

"Frankly, what you've just described sounds like an ordinary day for some of the teams at my company," said Dan, sighing.

"Now, what would happen if you had practiced and rehearsed together so you didn't have to fumble around as much?"

"We'd be able to find our way around the stage for starters," said Dan.

"You'd know the parts you had to play, you'd understand how they fit into the whole composition. Absolute Pitch would seem like an achievable goal, wouldn't it?"

"Sure," agreed Dan.

"See, when you prepare and rehearse, everyone works together more harmoniously. You become more effective at hitting the right tempo. You expand your capacity. That means you free up time."

"You're telling me that if our teams spend time rehearsing, we won't have less time to get stuff done but more time?"

"Case in point: years ago, we bought a smaller company that was making sonar systems for scientific research boats," said Michael, settling back comfortably in his chair. "They had a Use and Repair Manual that went with it, naturally.

"When we first acquired this business, that Use and Repair Manual would take thirteen months to produce. We launched our first new piece of equipment—and it wasn't until thirteen months later that the people using the equipment got the manual telling them how to use it or repair it!

"Every time the engineers made an improvement to the equipment, the manual had to be reviewed and rewritten. The slowness of

the process actually caused it to be even slower, which caused it to be slower still. That was because so many revisions and edits needed to be made to keep up with the frequent engineering advancements.

"Would you believe that by taking a brief time-out to uncover what was going wrong, we cut the time from thirteen months to six weeks?"

"Seriously?" asked Dan. "How did you do it?"

"It turned out that the people working on the manual were located in different buildings all over the city where this equipment was manufactured. So step one, we moved these people to be physically close to each other so that they could talk. We also scripted the work very carefully, setting out a plan for how the work would be completed within six weeks.

"While the engineering changed a lot in thirteen months, it didn't change that much in six weeks, so we didn't have to make endless rounds of revisions."

"That's amazing," said Dan. "You really did free up time."

"It gets better," said Michael. "We didn't quit rehearsing. Next, we dug down to get a better sense of the consumers—the people who were using this manual—and whether we were moving at their tempo. Turned out there were two audiences: the boat captains who used the sonar and the guys who repaired the equipment. So we split the manual in half. Now we're publishing two specific manuals, and we're able to do it in four weeks."

"You took the time you gained and put it into more rehearsals," observed Dan. "It's like investing money in the bank."

"Spot on, my friend," said Michael. "If you reinvest the time you gain from improvement into more rehearsal, it further improves the way you work. That frees up more time, which you can reinvest . . . You get the picture. Before you know it, you're on the pathway to continuous improvement."

7

TURNING A DRONE INTO A SYMPHONY

*D*an had been staring at the back of the same car for twenty minutes. As it rolled forward an inch or two then stopped, he would roll forward an inch or two then stop. The tight, heavy feeling in his head was only getting worse. Should he be worried about his blood pressure?

It didn't help that he always found this city one of the more uninspiring places that he had to travel to as part of his regular trips to the company's manufacturing plants. On the highway leading from the airport to where the plant was located, everything was a washed-out gray-brown: a tangle of elevated highways and concrete barriers and nondescript office buildings.

Dan and Michael were having their regular catch-up about Absolute Pitch on the phone, but Dan was beginning to think he probably should have let Michael's call go to voice mail until he was in a better mood.

"Everything okay, buddy?" Even over speakerphone, it was obvious that Michael had perceived the tension in Dan's voice.

"*Sorry, I'm just losing my patience here. I feel like I'm never going to get out of this traffic,*" *he replied.*

The drivers around him all looked bored as they stared into space. "*You know what? It's more than just the traffic, Michael. I feel like I'm stuck everywhere I turn. It's bugging me that you fixed that drama over the approval for the invitation, yet now we're dealing with a dispute over approval for yet another document. You heard about the e-mail war over that grant application, right?*"

"*I had heard about that,*" *Michael managed to say before Dan continued.*

"*Worse, I just about got laughed out of the room when I tried to talk to leadership in my company about improving our pulse-taking. Some of these people are like dinosaurs—they're going to get stuck in a bog while our competition moves on!*" *he said.* "*I don't know, maybe my company just isn't going to be suited to doing this.*"

"*Well, let's—*" *Michael started to respond, but Dan was only pausing for breath.*

"*And don't get me started on my boss,*" *he continued.* "*He doesn't understand compositions or harmony or tempo. We're coming at things from such different perspectives. Honestly, I think I'm going to have to wait for him to retire.*" *Dan stopped talking and gritted his teeth as someone pushed into his lane.*

"*Dan,*" *said Michael,* "*you've just told me the things you can't do.*"

"*Uh-huh.*"

"*Well, you can sit there all day long telling me what you can't do. What I want you to tell me is: what* can *you do?*"

Dan felt as though he'd just had cold water splashed on his face. "*Well, I . . . I . . .*" *Michael must have been leading up to a point; he always had a point. It just wasn't immediately clear to Dan.*

"*It's really not that complicated. Your ability to start enacting organizational improvements comes down to a few conditions. For* starters, do you have the guts—the gumption—to implement improvements in your teams?" Michael asked. "I believe you do."

"Thank you for your vote of confidence," replied Dan. The highway had just widened by two lanes, and the traffic jam in front of him began to break up. It was still slow, but at least he was moving now.

"Second, it's a question of how you deal with pockets of resistance. Everyone faces some resistance, by the way. But maybe there are ways you can work around them?"

"I hadn't thought of it like that," Dan said. "So far, I've been focusing on the obstacles to Absolute Pitch. I must admit I hadn't given any thought yet to the ways I might bypass them."

"If you sit down and formulate a strategy, I think you'll find you have more options than you realize," replied Michael. "And finally, don't underestimate your influence. When you talked about your ideas, Absolute Pitch immediately resonated with some people, didn't it? People who just 'got it' right off the bat?"

"You're right," agreed Dan. "It's just that without the whole—"

Michael cut this line of thinking short and said, "Has it occurred to you that you have at your disposal another very powerful way of influencing people? I know you can do it because any leader can do it: you can behave in the way that you want everyone else to behave."

"That certainly sounds like the right thing to do," Dan said, "but how will it change anything?"

"Let me answer that with another question: If you're going to get everyone on Absolute Pitch, you're going to need a cultural shift in your organization, right?"

"Definitely," Dan agreed.

"Well, what determines the culture of an organization?" Michael asked.

Dan had reached his exit and was leaving the clogged highway behind him. With the long curved exit ramp all to himself, he put his *foot on the accelerator as he thought about Michael's question. The tension started to leave his body; he always liked coming off the highway here because at the end of the ramp was a farm field. Today the field was planted with a deep green crop that had yellow flowers. The sky above the field was a huge expanse of blue with bright white puffy clouds on the horizon.* "Leadership," *he said finally.* "The way the leadership behaves is what determines the culture."

"Correct. Even if your boss and your peers don't behave in a manner that aligns with Absolute Pitch, you can. People are going to start saying, 'Wow, there's something different about Dan. He's really getting results. What's he doing, and can I do it too?' I'm not going to sugarcoat it: this may take time, and you may have hindrances. But you *will shift your company's culture."*

Whenever a group of people is introduced to the idea of organizational improvement, some of them will embrace it. But as Dan has just begun to learn, some people will feel indifferent, some will believe that it's not relevant to their organization, and some will reject it outright. These pockets of resistance maintain the state of "drone stagnation" that has developed in the organization.

In music, a drone is a sustained note that runs beneath a piece of music. In an organization, you can think of it as a monotonous background hum that signals stagnation has set in.

Drone stagnation: A state in which an organization is not improving, progressing, or moving forward.

In this chapter, we are going to look at how drone stagnation develops, why some people try to maintain it by resisting change, and how Absolute Pitch can succeed where other attempts at organizational improvement have failed.

Recognizing How Drone Stagnation Takes Hold

An orchestra conductor can hear immediately when something has gone awry during a performance—someone plays a wrong note or misses a beat, or someone plays too soft or too loud, too fast or slow.

If only it was that straightforward in other organizations. In businesses, nonprofits, schools, and hospitals all around the country, many people don't even recognize when something is abnormal about their organization's day-to-day running. That's because they have become so accustomed to dysfunction that the abnormal has become normal.

Because they do not have the constancy of purpose and clarity of vision of an Absolute Pitch organization, their work is dictated by circumstances rather than a plan. An ordinary day involves a series of things going wrong, one after another, which they work long and hard to fix.

In this environment, a leader goes in every morning knowing that their day is always going to be about fixing problems; what type of problems they will be fixing depends only on who happens to walk through their door. We call this the "Last Guy In Syndrome."

If the marketing manager was the last person coming to the door with problems, the leader works on solving marketing problems; if the last person was the operations manager, then it's operations problems that get solved; if it's someone from human resources at the door, they will work on personnel problems.

Rather than members of a harmonious ensemble playing a symphony together, in an organization such as this each person takes the opportunity to act like a rock star, doing an impromptu solo to solve the crisis of the moment. They work so hard to achieve short-term goals—such as finding temporary fixes to immediate troubles—that they don't step back and recognize the way they're working is not normal.

The organization tends to get stuck in a loop where they produce more of this behavior from people. That's because people are rewarded for fixing problems, so inevitably more problems are created.

With no way to tell abnormal from normal, sour notes go undetected. People may perceive their organization is living up to the expectations of their customers, consumers, and stake-holders when, in fact, it is not at all. Unable to see that they should make improvements to the way they carry out their work, they have reached the point of drone stagnation.

Finding a New "Normal"

To achieve standing ovations, an organization needs to be able to hear sour notes and correct them. That means the critical first step to getting out of drone stagnation and moving toward Absolute Pitch is to establish a new "normal."

There are leaders in many organizations that actually have worked very hard to try to establish a new normal. In fact, if you stay in almost any organization long enough, you are likely to witness numerous waves of change: reconfigurations of personnel, structure, work spaces, business plans, strategies, and work processes—all in an effort to establish "normal." Yet usually it remains elusive.

The key to success is to reset the organization's idea of normal to Absolute Pitch: the state when every member of the organization hits the right note every time, in unison and harmony, and people call for encores. With Absolute Pitch as the benchmark of normality, everyone in the organization knows they are aiming to follow a well-planned composition, to make sure everyone understands the parts they have to play, to get on the right tempo, and to hit the right chords to create harmony. When that is what they consider normal, people are able to recognize a sour note as abnormal. They become keenly aware of when they are not meeting the expectations of customers, consumers, or stakeholders. They are able to identify a problem as soon as it crops up and quickly get back to normal, rather than being trapped in a dysfunctional cycle of responding to crises as they arise.

Of course, it's not always easy to establish Absolute Pitch as the new normal. It requires effort, and it requires you to start looking at things in a different way. In an organization where people are acting like rock stars, it can be difficult to step back and say, "You know what? The way we're working isn't the way we should be working. We need to establish a new normal." This readjustment can be especially challenging in organizations that deal with a high level of variation in their work as it means calling on people to pause from reflexively responding every time conditions vary.

It takes guts to stop immediately responding to the first problem that walks in your door and instead pause, think about the problem, and prioritize it properly. In organizations that are stuck in crisis mode, this may almost feel like an impossible step to take. In reality, if you follow the principles of Absolute Pitch, you will have all the tools you need to make the switch. When you set Absolute Pitch as your "normal," you are grounded by a clear vision and purpose. You know what you believe in. You know what direction you are meant to be taking. This constancy of purpose gives you the decision-making criteria you need. It gives you the confidence and assurance to make the right choice: to not just respond to immediate, urgent problems but to prioritize finding long-term solutions and improvements that bring you closer to Absolute Pitch.

Introducing Absolute Pitch to the Organization

Once an organization has committed to the principles of Absolute Pitch, there is work to be done: The composition has to be thought through. Decisions need to be made about how teams will interact and carry out their work. Ways need to be found to get the teams engaging with one another harmoniously and working together at the tempo of the consumer.

When that conceptual work has been completed, it is time to put the ideas into action. This is when development and training programs become crucial. People cannot simply figure out how to adopt the principles of Absolute Pitch without guidance. The principles need to be taught, discussed, and practiced.

Still, there may be pockets of resistance that want to maintain drone stagnation. Stagnant water is very unappealing—just think of what grows in a pond in the summertime if there is no circulation in the water. It may seem odd that some members of an organization would prefer to maintain such a state, but the truth is, it can feel quite comfortable because to them the abnormal has become normal.

They may not even realize they have stopped moving forward. They go in each day, work hard, and do what they think is right; they believe they're playing their part very well. And they may be right—they could be the very best in the world at what they do.

Of course, being the best at what they do doesn't mean much if the organization has a shaky future because it has stagnated and is failing to please its customers, consumers, and stakeholders. Yet if people have been well rewarded and have had a successful tenure at the organization, they may feel they have a good reason for maintaining the status quo. They may purposely create drone stagnation because they feel that the shift to an Absolute Pitch approach will not be in their best interest. This is their attempt to preserve what they think is the ideal situation for them rather than looking at the big picture and asking, "How can I best participate in the organization moving forward?"

Removing Fear with a Growth Mind-Set

Instead of experiencing excitement at the prospect of receiving standing ovations, the people in an organization who try to maintain drone stagnation rather than embrace improvement may be fearful about what their future holds. To them, an organizational improvement program may be synonymous with staffing cuts.

Indeed, as we discussed in chapter 6, as an organization improves the way it works, it creates more capacity. As a result, at some point the organization will need fewer people—unless it simultaneously creates growth. So an Absolute Pitch organization channels its extra capacity into growth and further improvements. This leads to more capacity and still further growth and improvement.

Absolute Pitch companies choose a variety of growth paths. In tough economic times, some grow by finding new ways to better serve their customers, such as cutting lead times and getting products onto the market faster. Others grow by improving aspects of their performance that enable them to win market share from competitors.

For the individuals in organizations such as these, improvement is not a cause of anxiety. With a solid grounding in the principles of Absolute Pitch, they know that the part they play is important to the performance of their team and the organization's overall performance. They feel connected to the other people on their team and all the other teams in the organization. They know the answer to the question "What's in it for me?" A constancy of purpose underpins everything they do, and they are working toward a shared vision with shared values.

~

Dan Tries a New Approach

It was the start of a new day, and Dan was just about to sit down and review his list of work priorities. He was old school when it came to making lists; he used a pen and paper because there was nothing quite so satisfying as crossing off a completed item.

His list stretched halfway down the page, the items ranked from highest to lowest priority. All he'd managed to cross off were a few tasks toward the bottom. Frequently that was how his day ended. "Tomorrow's a new day," he always told himself. Yet that day never seemed to come because something critical would always pop up that had to be dealt with immediately.

As if on cue, just as he was lowering himself into his chair, Cathy appeared at his door to tell him about multiple urgent problems that had cropped up at their plants. As she went through them one by one, her face began to take on a puzzled look. Finally, she said, "Um, is everything okay, Dan?"

"Sure, why do you ask?"

"Well, it's just that you always write everything down in that notebook of yours," she said.

Dan glanced down at his list. Tomorrow had finally come, he decided. He and Cathy were never going to solve the root causes of the problems that kept popping up in their factories on a daily basis unless he got to the first few priorities on his list. They would just keep repeating this scene every morning.

Usually, Dan would have dropped whatever he was doing to take some of the problems off Cathy's plate because they seemed urgent. Then the warehouse manager or the purchasing manager would appear at the door with some equally urgent problems, and before he knew it, the day would be done. Actually, he used to think that a key measure of a successful day at work was how creatively and effectively he dealt with the curve balls thrown at him. But he was starting to see the world differently. Sure, he may help save the day if he threw away his composition, but where would the company be in a month's time? In six months' time? A year?

The only way to ensure a better future was to start dealing with the top-priority items on his list. And now that he stopped and looked at the situation from the standpoint of Absolute Pitch as his new "normal," he could see that the problems Cathy was talking about were not his first priority or even his second; they were more like his third, fourth, and fifth priorities.

What was it that Michael had said about changing the culture in an organization? Dan knew he had to model the behavior that he wanted to see in Cathy and everyone in his teams. "Thanks for the update, Cathy. I have every confidence that you can handle it. I have other priorities to attend to right now," he said.

"Oh, okay," said Cathy, sounding surprised. Uncertain, she wavered at the threshold of his office for a moment because this was not how their interaction usually played out.

Dan asked, "Out of interest, how much of your day do you think you spend dealing with crises?"

"Crises?" she asked. "I don't have to deal with all that many

crises. *Things break down. I find out what's broken, and I make sure they get fixed. I'm just doing my job."*

"So would you say that about 95 percent of the time you're responding to red signals?"

"Hmm, more like 99 percent, I'd say," she replied.

"Well, what if I said I think we could get to a point where we have consistent, effective processes and our plants run smoothly 99 percent of the time?"

Cathy snorted, then quickly said, "Oh, you're serious."

"If that was what we considered normal, whenever we got on amber, what do you think would happen?" he asked.

Cathy thought about it and then said, "I think we'd be better at spotting a minor problem and fixing it before it became a serious issue."

"We would immediately recognize when we'd slipped from normal performance to abnormal. People would stop the line and intervene to get things running smoothly again. And we would be able to consistently turn out excellent products that exceed our customers' and our users' expectations," Dan said.

Maybe his message had hit home. From the look in Cathy's eyes, Dan sensed she might have an inkling that it was time for a shift in what she accepted as an ordinary working day.

8

ENCORE, ENCORE!

O n the golf course at a fund-raising event, Dan had been lucky to meet Randy, one of the founders of a small community bank that held this fund-raiser each year. Like a lot of people in their town, Dan and his wife were loyal customers of the bank because their service was second to none.

Dan was always looking out for real-life examples of Absolute Pitch, and the bank achieved an encore performance almost every time he walked through their doors. So at the end of the round, he asked Randy if he could spare some time one day to share his experiences. That was how they came to be enjoying a burger in the diner across the road from one of the bank's four branches, on Main Street.

Randy had just filled in Dan on how he started his career working for a big financial institution, until he and a friend decided it was time to give customers something different. "We sat down and made a list of all the things that made other banks' performances bad and thought of all the ways we could do those things better," he said. "We developed our own business processes so that we could assure our customers of quick turnarounds and quick approvals. Another point of difference is that we decided to be a 'high-touch' bank, focused on customer service. We would create a better relationship between our employees and customers than you get in other banks."

"You know, I've noticed that. When I walk in, someone always addresses me by name and asks how my kids are. Before I know it, they've worked out what I need and have taken me over to the person who can help me. It's much friendlier than other banks and also way more streamlined," said Dan.

"I'm so glad to hear that," Randy replied. "From the outset, we decided our employees would be offered an ownership stake in the business. That's so they truly feel they're a part of the enterprise and have a lot invested in getting it right for our customers. And one of the reasons your experience is so streamlined is they've scripted out those interactions and practiced them."

The bank's employees had a genuine sense of being part of the wider orchestra, thought Dan. They had well-written compositions to follow, they knew the part they had to play and how it fitted in to the whole performance, and they spent time rehearsing too.

"It took several years of planning before we were ready to open the doors. We aimed to be a great regional bank that provided financing for real estate. We also planned to build a good trust department. Our long-term goal was to become a sizable bank with branches all over the state within a couple of decades," said Randy.

"Oh?" said Dan. "Small and personalized, that's how I think of the bank when I hear its name. I think of savings and checking accounts, mortgages and auto loans, investment accounts."

Randy chuckled. "As you can see, the game plan changed a lot. It's been a process of continual refinement."

"How did you know what path to take?" asked Dan.

"The changes we made were driven by listening to our customers and the marketplace and by being alert to shifts in the industry that were outside of our control," Randy replied.

"What kind of shifts?"

"Well, let's see—government policies changed, which meant it was better to keep the bank smaller and more customer-centric. Opportunities emerged in wealth management and other banking products and services. We realized we didn't need the same-sized branches as the bigger banks, so we moved locations," said Randy. "Now let me ask you something, Dan. How did you hear about the bank?"

"Um, let me think. You know, when we moved here, our neighbor told us about it."

Randy smiled. "Word of mouth turned out to be far more effective for our type of business than ads, so we cut our advertising dollars and spent more time and energy getting involved in the community."

"Like hosting golf days," added Dan. It was clear from Randy's story that he and the bank's cofounder had planned everything thoroughly before raising the baton. Then they had been highly perceptive conductors who listened carefully for ways to improve the performance once it was under way. "I've got to admit something to you. Back in '08, '09, I was worried you guys mightn't be able to weather the storm."

"We not only survived, we bounced back and prospered. In just a decade and a half we have built up about $170 million in assets in the bank. On the wealth management side, we've gone from $50 million to $700 million."

"All from staying on the drumbeat of treating people right, listening to the voice of the customer, providing high-touch service, and making sure everyone in the company knows they belong to something bigger than themselves," said Dan, counting off the key points with his fingers.

"That's it in a nutshell," agreed Randy. "And we will never stop doing those things, because we know improvement is an ongoing *process. You have to be looking out for whatever change is on the horizon or finding new ways to make your customers happy."*

"It's pretty inspiring to see you're still juiced about this fifteen years down the track," said Dan.

"You know that Absolute Pitch idea you were telling me about on the golf course the other day? Well, you could say we know what it's like to get encores," replied Randy. "Not every time, I'll admit. There are days when things don't go as planned. But once you know how good it feels to get an encore, it spurs you on to keep trying. You never want to settle for anything less."

The ultimate goal of an Absolute Pitch organization is to provide such exceptional products or services that everyone—customers, consumers, stakeholders, and people in the organization itself—gets to their feet to applaud and ask for more.

Encore: Recognition of an organization's exceptional performance from customers, consumers, stakeholders, and individuals within the organization, expressing their desire for the performance to continue.

Some of the ways that customers and consumers call for encores are by reordering, giving glowing reviews, or telling friends and family about their great experience. Shareholders may show their appreciation for a business's solid returns and good investment practices through further investment. Stakeholders in nonprofits may invest further money, time, or other resources into the organization. An outstanding performance by an individual or group within the organization may be rewarded and acknowledged by others in the organization.

Getting Encores, Not Just Pleasing Your Audience

To reach Absolute Pitch would mean to achieve perfection. This would require the perfect composition, tempo, harmony, and melody. A full complement of players would need to be performing at their peak. All the circumstances would have to be ideal.

A more familiar goal for most organizations is a pleasing performance. It's not perfect, but the organization meets its targets. The customers and consumers find it pleasing and may not notice the imperfections.

What makes Absolute Pitch organizations stand out from their competition is not that they achieve perfect performances every time. As Randy pointed out to Dan, even in exceptionally successful organizations things don't always go according to plan. What sets them apart is that they are not satisfied with giving a pleasing performance. They analyze the gap between their performance and what an Absolute

Pitch performance would sound like. They work continuously on closing that gap by changing the composition, rearranging the players they have on the stage, taking time out for rehearsals, and listening to the audience so they can match their tempo.

Absolute Pitch organizations strive to give performances that go far beyond the level of pleasing so that they truly wow their customers and consumers. Think of the difference between the enjoyable symphony performance Michael took Dan to first and the truly exceptional orchestra the following week that had the whole audience on their feet thunderously applauding.

When an organization takes its performance beyond the level of pleasing, its customers and consumers call for encores —they want more of the product or service the organization provides. They also become promoters of the organization. For instance, after the exceptional orchestra performance Dan went to, the next day at work he told several people about how fantastic it was, and they bought tickets for that evening's performance.

Creating this type of viral marketing buzz should be a goal for every organization. At Randy's bank, that means cultivating positive word of mouth in the community, which results in more customers opening accounts. At Dan's company, it means improving performance to the point where users recommend their medical devices to others, leading to higher sales.

An Absolute Pitch organization knows it's important to create a viral marketing buzz not only externally among the audience but also internally within the organization. When people perform especially well, the organization makes sure the achievement is celebrated. This sets off a chain of excitement that has people raring to go and saying, "That was great! How do we do it again?"

Recognizing an Absolute Pitch Performance

As an audience member, you might have a very clear sense of the difference between a pleasing performance and an Absolute Pitch performance. You probably have been to quite a number of concerts that were enjoyable but have experienced only a handful of truly memorable ones that you wished would never end. As an audience member looking on, it can be easy to see the difference. For the players on the stage, it tends to be much harder to make that distinction.

Similarly, it is difficult for an organization to tell whether they are giving a pleasing performance or an Absolute Pitch performance. In an ideal world, the conductor—the leader of the organization—would be so tuned in that they could hear tiny sour notes that could wind up being big problems. Yet most organizations are so busy dealing with day-to-day concerns that the conductor may not notice sour notes.

This is why Absolute Pitch organizations often bring in trained experts to assess performance. They can notice and point out problems of which the organization was unaware, stimulate a new discussion within the organization, and suggest improvements that will bring different, better results.

A School System Achieves Encore Performances

"Thanks for taking the time to talk to us," said Dan's wife, Jill, as she and Dan sat down across the desk from the school principal, Maria.

"You are so welcome," she replied, smiling warmly. "I'm always happy to talk about what we can do to improve the future of our kids."

Jill had heard about the outstanding academic results children were getting in the district's charter school system. As their eldest daughter would be heading to high school in a couple of years, she set up this meeting with the principal. The more Jill and Dan had researched the charter schools, the more Dan had come to think that this might be another example of an organization working toward Absolute Pitch.

He and Jill were concerned about what lay ahead for their daughter and son. Even now, kids were graduating from college with up to $100,000 in debt, struggling to pay it back from low starting salaries. And every time rankings came out, the country's academic achievement in important subjects like math and science was shown to be slipping behind other nations around the world. Dan and Jill were worried their children might graduate unprepared to compete in the global marketplace.

The charter school association would really need constancy of purpose to get the education system's drone stagnation moving again. "Maria, I can imagine there are a lot of different interested parties involved in your schools—parents, students, teachers. Can I ask, what are the values you all share?"

"Sure. From the beginning, we knew we had to involve everyone in the discussion and come together around a central purpose. Ours is to graduate students who are able to contribute positively to the community." Dan and Jill nodded their approval. Maria continued, "As you pointed out, Dan, there are so many stakeholders and so many factors to consider in an educational system. You need the right curriculum. You need students who are conditioned and willing to learn. You need the contributions of parents and teachers, administrators, the community."

"But can all of those parties ever do a good job of working together?" asked Jill. "Going by our experiences at our kids' schools, they're usually pulling in completely different directions."

"Well, once we decided on a mission that we were all committed to, something pretty great happened: all those different stakeholders felt like they were part of something bigger," said Maria. "Now they give their absolute best because they feel they have something important to contribute to an important mission."

If the charter school association was hoping to achieve Absolute Pitch, they would need decision-making criteria so that their actions were aligned with the values of everyone involved in the schools, thought Dan. "There must have been a huge amount of choices you had to make when you were planning the school. How did you know what was best?" he asked.

"There were months of discussion about what was valued by parents, students, teachers, school staff, community members— everyone with a stake in the school system. There were no closed-door meetings. Everything was done in a public forum, open to anyone who wanted to participate. From those discussions, we agreed on key criteria and processes that became the school's charter," Maria replied. "Whenever a contentious decision needs to made, we can return to those criteria so we know if we're making a choice that is in everyone's interests."

"I've heard so many great things about your school from other parents. What do you do that's so different from other schools?" Jill asked.

"I think the biggest difference you will find here is that we put a lot more emphasis on listening to our parents and students. We engage with them to find out what they need and want. That informs our curriculum and the way we deliver education," said Maria. "Of course, not everyone likes that idea because they feel authority is *being taken away from teachers and bureaucrats. But given our results, it's becoming hard for them to argue with our approach."*

"I heard that some of your students are graduating with two years of college credits. Is that really true?" Jill asked.

"You heard right," said Maria, nodding.

"So, a student could graduate at eighteen with two years of college credits. That would cut their debt in half and put them ahead of everyone else their age when they finish college and start looking for a job," mused Dan.

"And what we've found is that most of the students who've taken this path have ended up getting degrees that lead to higher-paying jobs, such as the sciences and engineering," continued Maria.

"Which means whatever college debt they do end up with, it's likely to yield a better return on their investment," Jill added.

The schools had achieved impressive results, but Dan wondered whether they had the same attitude to continual improvement as Randy, the cofounder of the community bank. "You've achieved a lot. What's next?" he asked Maria.

"Up until now, our organization's focus has mostly been on engaging everyone and getting them to work together in harmony," she said. "But we've been talking about how in the future we need to start addressing other elements of a good education—like building new schools so that we keep up with the changing demographics here. We need to look at improving the efficiency of our buildings and our operations too."

"I was reading the other day about one school district that went out and studied how big tech companies like Apple and Google work and then planned their new schools based on what they learned," Dan shared. "These schools are going to emphasize project-based learning. They actually designed the buildings to create the best environment for that, instead of building the school first and making the education system fit into it. Things have changed since we were kids!"

"That's right, society is changing all the time," said Maria. "Testing requirements change. So do college requirements and vocational needs. We have to keep moving forward and improving, while staying focused on our mission: to graduate students who are able to contribute positively to the community."

Jill and Dan shared a glance and nodded at each other. Turning to Maria, Jill said, "Can we put Laura and Tom on the waiting list? I'm assuming there's a waiting list."

"That's right, we have a lot of interest from new parents and from parents bringing their whole family through our system," said Maria, pulling a form out of her drawer and pushing it across the desk to Jill and Dan.

They were giving students, parents, community stakeholders—and even their teachers—a better service, Dan thought. No wonder people were calling for encores!

EPILOGUE

"Thank you, everyone, for being here," said Dan as he looked around the table at the committee members who'd gathered for the monthly meeting of the nonprofit he served. This was only his third meeting since being voted into the role of chair, and the feeling of honor and responsibility was still fresh. Across the table was Michael. In the past he'd filled almost every executive position in his many years on the board, and Dan was grateful for his experience and support.

There was one empty chair, but it was soon filled by the most recent addition to the board, Sofia, who rushed in looking flustered and uttered a quick apology as she took her seat. Dan gave her an understanding smile. After all, just a little over a year ago the idea of him arriving at a committee meeting on time had been laughable.

So much had changed. It took persistence, but Dan had eventually got enough people at work to seriously consider his ideas about changing when and how the company took its pulse. After many of his suggestions were implemented, they had gradually got back on track and launched into their two new markets.

Next they had plans to grow the company by introducing some innovative product lines. But they knew they would probably repeat past mistakes unless they took a good look at the way the company operated. So Dan was appointed as head of a special team to review and improve several of the company's key processes. Meanwhile Cathy, the manager Dan had fought fires with every morning, was leading a team to get clarity on the organization's vision.

Sure, there were pockets of resistance at work—people who wanted things to stay the way they were—but on the whole there were fewer crises and rock-star performances. Best of all, people generally seemed more engaged in their work, and the organization was retaining more good staff.

Dan and Michael still sometimes got together to chat about how to bring organizations to Absolute Pitch. But more often when they got together now, it was for fly-fishing. As they walked to their cars after the committee meeting, they started tossing dates around for their next trip. Standing by his car in the parking lot, Dan checked the calendar on his tablet. Then he saw his pictures from the beach vacation he'd just taken with his family. He showed Michael a couple of them, and the older man laughed and placed his hand on Dan's shoulder. "Look how far you've come," he said.

"I've still got a ways to go," Dan replied.

"Don't we all?" said Michael.

Dan nodded and said, "I see endless potential for change everywhere."

There would always be more improvements to make at work. He had already discussed with Michael his plans to lead positive change at the nonprofit. After seeing the look on Sofia's face tonight as she arrived from the law office where she was a partner, he realized that he also had worthwhile insights to share with individuals he met. Not to mention that any organization he got involved with in the future —schools, hospitals, churches—could benefit.

"I look around and see there are just so many places where there's disharmony and stagnation," Dan told Michael. *Suddenly he straightened up and smiled. "Then I imagine all the ways I can help create harmony and get things moving forward again."*

We hope you've enjoyed this story and decide pursue harmony and synchronization in your organization — it can happen!

For more information about Absolute Pitch or to inquire about bringing Absolute Pitch to your organization, visit us at www.AbsolutePitchBook.com.

GLOSSARY OF TERMS

- **Absolute Pitch:** When every member of an organization hits the right note every time, in unison and harmony. This results in encore performances.
- **Chord:** The actions of two or more individuals or groups within an organization that together produce a harmonious outcome.
- **Composition:** An organization's plan for how tasks will be performed.
- **Consumers:** The people who use an organization's products or services.
- **Customers:** The people who acquire an organization's products or services. Customers include people who buy from businesses and people who access the products or services of a nonprofit organization free of charge.
- **Drone stagnation:** A state in which an organization is not improving, progressing, or moving forward.

- **Dynamics:** Changes in the intensity of the work performed in an organization.
- **Encore:** Recognition of an organization's exceptional performance from customers, consumers, stakeholders, and individuals within the organization, expressing their desire for the performance to continue.
- **Ensemble performance:** When an individual performs in a way that contributes to and benefits the whole organization.
- **Impromptu performance:** Work performed without a plan or with disregard for the plan.
- **Improvisation:** A pause in an organization's performance, creating an environment for discovery in which individuals or teams can safely try out new approaches to their work.
- **Medley:** A sequence of three or more teams' outcomes that together lead to a bigger overall outcome.
- **Melody:** The pattern of behavior of individuals that forms the organization's output.
- **Meter:** The units of work completed in a set time period.
- **Organization:** Any group with a common purpose —for instance, a small or medium-sized business, large corporation, government body, hospital, school, church, nonprofit, or social or community group.
- **Pulse-taking:** A management system that monitors the "heartbeat" of the organization to check whether it is achieving the right tempo, melody, and chords to produce the desired outcome.

- **Rehearsal:** The time individuals spend practicing the behaviors that lead to Absolute Pitch.
- **Stakeholders:** People who have something at stake in the organization. For a company, this may mean shareholders or owners. For other organizations, it may mean people who are impacted by the organization, such as community members.
- **Tempo:** The pace at which an organization needs to move in order to meet its consumers' demands.
- **Unison:** People in an organization working in sync with one another and in alignment with the values of the organization, customers, consumers, and stakeholders.

ABOUT THE AUTHORS

Robert Blaha helps organizations streamline their operations, cut costs, and boost productivity. After a successful career in senior management at major corporations including Ford and Monsanto, he founded consultancy firm Human Capital Associates and he continues to be its president. He also co-founded Integrity Bank & Trust in Colorado Springs and is the vice chairman of its board of directors.

An internationally sought speaker on leadership and organizational change, he is the author of three books: *Beyond Survival*, *The Archer Chronicles*, and *The Lean 6 Sigma Accelerator*.

He has been featured in *Quality Digest, Human Resource*

Management, Chief Learning Officer, Industry Week, and *Harvard Management Update.*

Robert is active in the school choice movement and has served on the boards of foster care and adoption organization Hope & Home and USA Boxing.

Contact Robert at rblaha-hcaleadership@hca.com

Bruce Thompson specializes in bringing harmony to businesses to make them more efficient and effective. He is the founder and president of SLT Consulting, an industry leader in business improvement and demand generation. The principles he applies have delivered results for some of the world's biggest corporations in the fields of healthcare, the military, aerospace, the automotive industry, and consumer packaged goods.

Since 2000 Bruce has been a Shingo examiner for the Shingo Institute at the Jon M. Huntsman School of Business. He also served on the committee developing Lean Certification Standards for the Association for Manufacturing Excellence and the Shingo Institute.

Bruce draws on almost three decades of management experience across a spectrum ranging from manufacturing and service through to product development, process analysis, quality, and operations.

Contact Bruce at B.Thompson@slt-llc.com

For more information Absolute Pitch, visit us at www.Absolute-PitchBook.com.